The British Sel

Arthur Eperon is one of the most experienced and best known travel writers in Europe. Since leaving the RAF in 1945 he has worked as a journalist in various capacities, often involving travel. He has concentrated on travel writing for the past twenty-five years and contributed to many publications including *The Times, Daily Telegraph, New York Times, Woman's Own, Popular Motoring* and the *TV Times.* He has appeared on radio and television and for five years ⟨...⟩ its food and wine, as a result of innumerable visits there over the last forty years. In 1974 he won the Prix des Provinces de France, the annual French award for travel writing.

He has been exploring Britain since he first set out with a back-pack tent over fifty years ago.

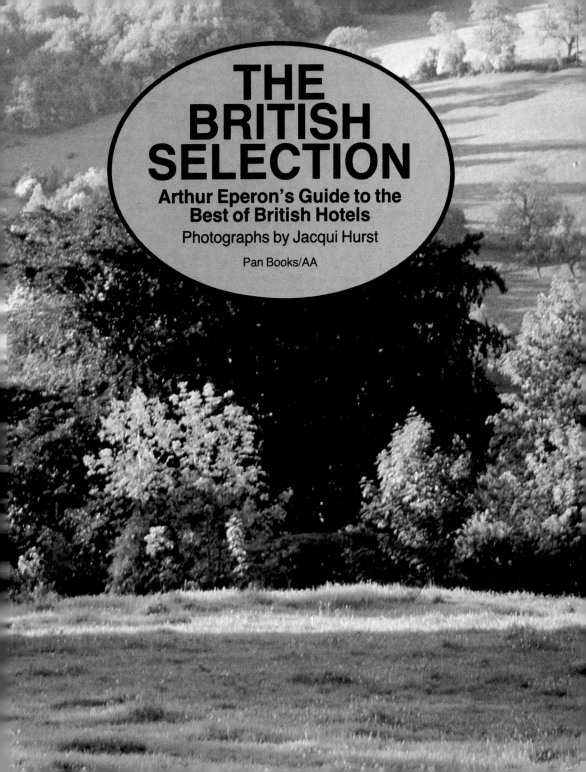

THE BRITISH SELECTION

Arthur Eperon's Guide to the Best of British Hotels

Photographs by Jacqui Hurst

Pan Books/AA

Also by Arthur Eperon
in Pan Books

Travellers' France
Encore Travellers' France
Le Weekend
The French Selection
Travellers' Britain
Travellers' Italy
(in association with the BBC)

First published 1985 by
Pan Books Ltd,
Cavaye Place, London SW10 9PG
and the Automobile Association
Fanum House, Basing View,
Basingstoke, Hampshire RG21 2EA
9 8 7 6 5 4 3 2 1
© Arthur Eperon 1985
Photographs © Jacqui Hurst 1985
Drawings © Sue Dray 1985
The maps are produced by the
Cartographic Department of the
Automobile Association
and are based upon Ordnance
Survey maps with the permission
of the Controller of Her Majesty's
Stationery Office.
Crown copyright reserved.
Designed by Peter Holroyd
Photoset by
Parker Typesetting Service,
Leicester
Printed in Spain by
Mateu Cromo Artes Graficas S.A.,
Madrid

ISBN 0 330 29104 1 (Pan
paperback)
ISBN 0 330 29466 0 (Pan
hardback)
ISBN 0 86145 347 6 (AA
paperback)
ISBN 0 86145 371 9 (AA
hardback)
AA reference 57752

THE SELECTION

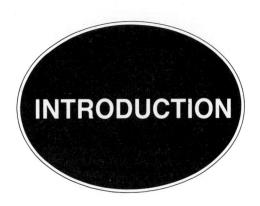

INTRODUCTION

An Italian chef working in a London restaurant despised all British cooking and British dishes. Nevertheless, he was told by the owner, he must put some traditional British dishes on his menu. I was lunching there when he introduced his 'Old English steak and kidney pie'. It was a cottage pie, topped with creamed potatoes, with the steak and kidney minced together underneath – reeking of oregano and garlic.

Despite the efforts of our tourist authorities over the past fifteen years, most people are still abysmally ignorant about the standards of British cooking and British hotels. Foreigners might be forgiven for not knowing that we now have hundreds of family-run country hotels which compare with any in the world for comfort, atmosphere, friendly service and facilities, and with most for food. I was not surprised when French hotelkeepers who know only London asked how I could find fifty hotels in Britain good enough for this book. But when someone important in

the London publishing world said the same, I realized that it was time that the book was written. 'I know a hundred already,' I said rather snootily. And the experts of the AA backed me up on this. I am delighted to have the AA approval of my book, for I have come to respect the judgement of their professional inspectors more and more in recent years.

British hotels and food have been judged for far too long on the prices and mass-catering in our big cities. On our way round this year both Barbara and I were amused at the wide-eyed amazement of American visitors when they were served magnificent lightly-cooked vegetables straight from the local market or often from the hotel's own garden. They had been brought up on their fathers' horror stories of British wartime mass cooking during rationing and the extraordinarily misleading comments in US magazines and newspapers, stories of soggy cabbage and sprouts, tinned peas, sauceless cauliflower, superannuated beans, tasteless jumbo-marrows – not to mention cardboard steaks and reheated roasts.

Guests from the US did have one valid complaint – the shortage of big imaginative salads in many country hotels where the rest of the meals are excellent. Maybe it is because our vegetables are so fresh, good and plentiful that we still eat far fewer salads than the Americans, whose vegetables are more likely to have come from a freezer than direct from a farm.

As with *The French Selection*, Barbara and I started with a list of more than 150 hotels which we knew or which had been highly recommended to us. We stayed and ate at all of them, some for the first time, some for the twentieth. We were looking for tranquil country hotels with individuality and atmosphere, preferably owned and run by a family. I should like to stress, as I did with France, that the ones which we have chosen are not necessarily among the most luxurious or efficient hotels I know, with gastronomic meals. Although a few are in the expensive luxury class, we have had to be particularly careful in Britain not to fall for too many of these. Bedrooms in British hotels are still much dearer than in France and our expensive hotels are still a lot more expensive than theirs.

Again, I have chosen the hotels because I like them. Most are in lovely or interesting surroundings, many have beautiful gardens, some have charming parks. They are all comfortable, some have beautiful old furniture. They have good cooking and most have interesting wines. They are run by friendly people. Most important, whatever their price, they are all good value.

As with France, we had to leave out some good ones because there were a lot in the same area. This was true particularly of the Bath area, Somerset, Cornwall, the Lake District, the Cotswolds and the centre of Scotland.

Twenty-five years ago when I was travel editor of a big group of magazines and newspapers my bosses insisted that I spent at least four months of the year touring Britain. I found a lot of pretty, charming, friendly country hotels in those days. But most seemed to be run as a hobby. They had 'good plain cooking' by a lady from the village, and plumbing down the corridor from your bedroom. The improvement since is astonishing and still not fully appreciated. There are a mere handful of bedrooms in the hotels I have chosen without their own bathrooms and the standard of bathrooms is excellent. Bedroom furnishing and decoration used to be the weak spot of smaller hotels here. Not any more. Some of the décor and colour schemes are almost inspired. And the thought, research and hard work – not to mention money – which some owners have put into restoring historic old stately homes and converting them into hotels deserves national recognition. Only the French have done this on anything like the scale that our hotel owners have done, and the French owners were given much more government aid.

Many of these new owners are not professional hotelkeepers. They were executives, accountants or directors of successful companies, either edged out by a take-over or who tired of

rushing round the world living out of a suitcase. They have applied business know-how and organization to their new job with great success. Either they or their wives have been to cookery school, so that even if they employ a chef, they know what is going on in the kitchen. Then there is a new generation of trained chef – managers who are more

treat eating as refuelling, those who expect to knock back a three-course meal and coffee in 40 minutes dead and get irritable at the slightest delay. These hotels are for people prepared to wait ten to fifteen minutes between courses to ensure that all their food is cooked fresh, not factory-packed, portioned and frozen, then rushed through a micro-oven.

A prolific travel writer said recently that he never followed any guide books which included food or restaurants because food was so much a matter of personal taste. Indeed. And that is why I think it is important to describe what sort of dishes an hotel offers. I would not want to arrive to find that an hotel had gone over completely to the recently-fashionable Nouvelle Cuisine or even entirely to what is called 'light modern' cooking. I do want to know whether I am going to get plenty of vegetables or not, whether I can have a roast if I want one, and so on. There are so many fashions and theories in cooking these days that I do not think it enough any more just to recommend restaurants without saying why or giving some idea of what they offer. I have tried where possible to choose hotels at which two or three people with different tastes can each find a meal they like.

Personally, I think that menus should change with the seasons, not the fashions. Nouvelle Cuisine, which had some enthusiastic fans here among the wealthier gourmets, never caught on in the north of England, for instance, or Scotland, where most people want a plateful of meat and mounds of fresh vegetables around them, not slivers for décor. Though the French grow the most delightful vegetables, some of the chefs are using them so sparingly that Britain is fast becoming the land of the best vegetables. Although I like them very lightly cooked, I am glad that many chefs in the hotels I have chosen offer on the menu card to cook them longer if a guest wishes. Each to his taste.

Our chefs may not quite have reached the standard of the best French chefs, but they do have a more liberal attitude to cooking. You may well find ducks breasts in strawberry sauce on the menu next to steak and kidney pie (one of the great dishes of the world), and not only classical and modern dishes side by side but Italian, Chinese and old local English or Scottish dishes. Incidentally, a lot of those modern sauces using ginger, mint, honey, elderberry, and fruit vinegars are versions of old sauces dating back to Elizabethan days.

A master of both classical and modern cooking is young Murdo MacSween, one of the best chefs in Britain, now at Oakley Court Hotel, Windsor. Of Nouvelle Cuisine he says, 'That is a phase we all went through. But it did encourage a lot of chefs to get away from the heavy-handedness of the more classic dishes and also led to a great deal more competition among us.'

A current danger is that the

professional than older generations and have moved around the world getting experience.

It is said that the British resent serving other people. That is simply not true about young people. We found the service in these country hotels friendly but efficient, caring but not hurrying. The hotels would not please people who

lucrative health food industry may turn healthy eating into faddy eating. A few people I have met seem so obsessed about diet and fitness that they seem likely to worry themselves into ulcers or at least depression. I am not joking, either. But some calorie-watchers do make me laugh. They choose fruit juice for starters, the lightest main course with a little spinach, perhaps, and definitely no bread or potatoes. Then they have a dessert of calorie-loaded cheesecake, gâteau, pastries or ice cream.

For my taste, some chefs even in Britain go too far in undercooking meat and fowl. Roast beef red in the middle — yes, of course. But there is no rule which says that lamb should be pink-raw near the bone just because Paris decreed it some years ago, and as for semi-raw duck — it is time we all sent it back for more cooking, unless you like fibrous chewing gum. I was even offered a pink pork chop at one hotel, not in this book. That is dangerous. And health food fadders are trying to start a fashion for half-raw white fish because some Chinese eat it that way. Some Chinese, it seems, live for 120 years but I was assured in Hong Kong that the expectation of life in China is way below ours.

Producing only a small amount of wine, we are far less prejudiced in our tastes than big wine producing countries, and visitors from abroad are often amazed at the variety in our wine lists. This is particularly helpful at present. Recently weather conditions have stripped many vineyards all over France and in Italy and Germany. I know one good Muscadet grower who lost 80 per cent of his crop in 1985, stripped by gales then hit by frost. Bordeaux, particularly St Emilion, has had two bad years in succession. Add the high prices which Americans have been paying for Burgundy with their strong dollars, and we can expect better-known wines to get a lot dearer.

There are some truly great wines on most of the hotel lists, but prices have got way past anything I could pay. So I have picked mostly cheaper or middle-priced wines. I think that we shall be making a lot of new friends among wines soon — wines from Cahors, from down the Rhône and Ardèche to areas like Bandol and Roussillon, taking in the Rhône wines of the Vaucluse. The wines of the far south of France have been improved enormously by replanting and better vinification over the past twenty years. So have wines of Rioja and Penedes in Spain. A lot of people forced to switch to them will be surprised at their flavour, bouquet and grapiness, not to mention their strength. And I think that Italian wines will regain their popularity because of price, especially good Chianti Classico Riserva and Valpolicella.

Even with some of my own favourite hotels, I am sad at the high mark up on wine in their restaurants. In many cases, the wines are 300 per cent dearer than their wholesale price. I know that the same is happening in some French restaurants, but we have to pay a punitive tax, too. In the long run, these high prices will simply mean that people will stick to the cheapest house wines and the hotel will suffer. There are some splendid exceptions of hotels selling lovely older wines well below the London auction prices.

I regret that many of my hotels have no lifts. Most are only two storeys high, few

over three. The problem is that they are nearly all very old houses, many historic, and it would be impossible to put in a lift without ruining a superb staircase, perhaps, or a fine entrance hall. There is less excuse for not having outside-call telephones in bedrooms, although that is expensive for small hotels.

There is a strange travel snobbery against teas-made machines in bedrooms. True, I would rather have a real maid to awaken me in the morning but you do not *have* to use these machines. Any hotel will bring you tea to your room if you ask.

The return to popularity of the 'short-break' of two or three days is an excellent trend. It means that the British might once again know as much about their own country as about Spain or France. I suspect that the more-stringent drinking and driving laws are partly responsible. Instead of going out to wine and dine once a week, a lot of people are taking a weekend away once a month or so.

Nearly all the hotels in this book have special terms for

short breaks, much below their normal prices. These may be seasonal or continue through the year. Some have theme weekends, too, for wine tasting, gourmet meals, music, flower arranging, visiting stately homes or lovely gardens and all sorts of other pastimes. If you think you would fancy a short break at any of these hotels, write to them and get on their mailing list for special offers.

The hotels I have chosen cover a fairly wide price range. Please do not expect the same luxurious standards from the simpler cheaper ones as from 'Relais et Château' hotels such as Chewton Glen, Lygon Arms and Sharrow Bay. I say this only because a few readers of *The French Selection* have expected too much of hotels which I have plainly stated are fairly simple. Position, views, atmosphere and pretty gardens weigh heavily with me. But I think that you will find that the people owning these hotels and those working with them, really do *care* about your comfort and happiness.

I hope that you will visit several of them and enjoy yourself in your own way.

Although photographs of Langley House, Wiveliscombe,
Somerset, appear on the cover of The British Selection, *the hotel*
could unfortunately not be included in the book because it
changed hands at the time of going to press.

The Airds Hotel

The Airds Hotel
Port Appin, Appin,
Argyllshire, Scotland
PA38 4DF (take A85, then
A828 N from Oban; then a
narrow lane left after
Creagan).
Telephone: Appin (063 173)
236.
DBB (including dinner) D, E;
SBB (including dinner) B.
Dinner C.
Bar lunch.
Closed December, January,
February. Reductions up to 75
per cent for children under 14
sharing parents' room.
Dogs accepted at proprietor's
discretion.
No credit cards.

From the sunlounge of this low white old ferry inn you can look down on the twisty shore of Loch Linnhe, across the long lean isle of Lismore and the little lumpy isle of Shuna to the mauve and green Morvern mountains – a lovely view at any time and magnificent when the sun sets in a blaze of red and gold. Here is peace and beauty without lifelessness.

Airds has long been one of our favourite spots in Scotland since we found it on a trip out from the nearby fishing port and beach resort of Oban. Yearly, Eric and Betty Allen have improved the rooms, added charming and helpful touches, and made more friends. The two big lounges are not only comfortable and attractive but have some higher, upright armchairs for old bones like mine.

You can take an aperitif or tea in the sunlounge or in a little bar, cosy in winter.

Over the road is a terrace with a colourful garden sloping to the loch shore. When the weather's good you can hire boats for exploring the coast.

Eric Allen, who gave up an important job in marketing in Edinburgh to plunge into hotel-keeping, is an uncommonly welcoming host – in a kilt, of course. Built around 1700, Airds was a very ordinary little inn until the Allens transformed it into a delightful, informal little hotel without destroying its old-inn atmosphere, and made it renowned for its food.

Food & Drink

A meal at the Airds is sheer pleasure. The dining room has views across the loch. Table settings are immaculate, with shining silver and glass, iced water, and fresh flowers. The smiling young girls in white blouses and tartan skirts are polite, friendly and quiet. Meals are lovingly made of the freshest local food of top quality, carefully cooked. Betty Allen must be one of the best self-taught cooks in the business. She makes traditional Scottish dishes with enough of modern cooking to lighten

them just a little. No wonder that a new official Scottish eating guide made her its first Chef of the Year.

Go behind the hotel to the big kitchen garden and you will see one of her secrets. The rows of vegetables look perfect. A huge plastic-covered horticultural frame keeps off early frosts, then is opened to the elements. I tried mange-tout peas raw from the rows, then later cooked to crisp tenderness by Betty, and I have not tasted better here or in France. New Scottish potatoes, tiny young carrots – all delicious and served in generous portions.

Haggis with creamed swede was a starter on my last visit. I cannot look a haggis in the eye. So I chose a superb terrine of turbot and scallops, both from Oban fishing boats. There is a fine choice of fish around here and Bettty has a way with it. Her mousseline of scallops is delicious, her sole with prawns and white wine sauce as good, and she has a dozen ways with Loch Awe trout and wild salmon. Her soups are very tempting – courgette and rosemary, for instance, and slightly sharp celery and tomato. And she has a fine variety of sauces for her dishes of Scottish lamb, beef, venison, saddle of hare and

free-range chickens.

I rarely order ice-cream but would hate to have missed her Scottish raspberry and Drambuie version. The choice of sweets is mouthwatering.

Betty makes superb bread, and breakfasts include eggs from their own free-range chickens.

Eric has bought his wines so shrewdly over the past years and is so reasonable in his mark-up that one famous wine writer quoted his prices for such great wines as Cheval Blanc St Emilion, La Mission Haut Brion, Château Margaux, Latour, Richebourg as being well below auction prices. But his list of more than 200 bottles and 70 half-bottles has a wide range of wines from £6 a bottle, some excellent and most-reasonably-priced middle-range clarets, such as fifth-growth Château Haut Batailley from Pauillac, a very fair list of Rhône wines, a good list from Germany, and in white Loire wines, one of the two Grand Cru Savennières from Anjou – the redoubtable Madame Joly's Clos de la Coulée de Serrant.

A good hotel for wine-lovers, too. You dine at 8 o'clock – one sitting to ensure fresh cooking.

Appin is the land of Robert Louis Stevenson's story Kidnapped. James Stewart, wrongly hanged for murdering Colin Campbell, Government factor for the Stewart estates forfeited after the Battle of Culloden in 1745, has a memorial at the spot where he was hanged, by the bridge at Ballachulish on A828 to Fort William. The Stewarts were Jacobites. So were the Macdonalds, who lived around Loch Leven, fifteen miles NE of Port Appin. The fearsome, sunless Glen Coe, with bare high black rock peaks, was the stage for the Glen Coe massacre, when in 1692 the Campbell Clan militia, after enjoying twelve days feasting as guests of the Macdonalds, slaughtered their hosts – men, women and children. Nearer Appin from the same road you can see, on a little isle among sandflats, Castle Stalker, a Stewart hunting lodge used by James IV before the Battle of Flodden. 28m SE of Fort William is Ben Nevis, highest peak in Britain (4406ft).

A small ferry for passengers only sails from Port Appin to the isle of Lismore, from which St Moluag spread Christianity about 560AD. It is ten miles long with one narrow road and you can take your car by ferry from Oban (23m S). From Oban you can also sail to the lovely isle of Mull (Craignure – 45 minutes) – visit Torosay Castle with glorious gardens, Duart Castle, with Maclean relics and a Scouting exhibition, and drive to Tobermory, a charming yachting centre with legends of sunken Spanish treasure from the Armada. Also boats go to Staffa, where the enormous Fingal's Cave inspired Mendelssohn's Hebrides Overture. By passenger ferry from Mull you can reach Iona, Holy isle of St Columba and burial place of Kings from Norway, Ireland and Scotland, including Macbeth and Duncan.

You either hate or love Oban. An animated seaside resort, fishing port, great boating centre, and with a Victorian folly of an unfinished copy of Rome's Colosseum, it has life and charm for me.

A real hideout – they'll never find you here!

BALCARY BAY HOTEL

**Balcary Bay Hotel
Auchencairn,
Near Castle Douglas,
Kirkcudbrightshire,
Scotland DG7 1QZ.
Telephone: Auchencairn (055
664) 217.
DBB A–C (very seasonal);
SBB A.
Some rooms do not have
private bathrooms.
Dinner A–C.
Closed January to mid-
February.
Credit cards: Euro, Visa,
Diners (not Amex).**

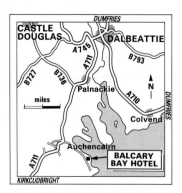

With only its back lawns divid-ing it from an enchanting protected bay, this pretty, un-assuming hotel is in one of my favourite parts of Britain – beau-tiful Dumfries and Galloway.

It has fewer facilities and less luxury than almost all the other hotels I have chosen – four rooms do not have private bathrooms – but it is also about the cheapest and we have great affection for it.

Galloway was almost undis-covered when I first found it in the 1940s and is still unclut-tered and uncrowded. But people drive around it on their way, perhaps, to Ayr and what is called the 'Burns Country' a little further north, are instantly captivated and rush back to try to buy a retirement home! One lure is the climate. Like Cornwall and the Isle of Man, it is washed by the Gulf Stream and semi-tropical plants grow here. Its secretive little fishing villages remind me of the Cornwall I knew as a child – with very few visitors. And here the hinterland has beautiful hills and forests, almost empty of people but rich in wildlife, lochs and rivers rich in fish.

The house was built in 1625. It looks across Balcary Bay to Hestan Isle, for centuries a smugglers' haunt, along the Solway coast and across to the Cumbrian Hills in England. A firm of shippers called Clark, Quirk and Crane bought the hotel in 1645 to use as head-quarters and warehouse for smuggled goods. These were stored in underground pas-sages reached behind a fire-place in the cellars.

Now the cellars are a bar called Raiders Cave. The tower above makes a charming lounge with bay windows looking out to sea, and the large reception lounge is beamed. Most bedrooms are big and light, with large windows and sea views. The smaller ones are at the front, away from the sea.

The hotel is now being run by a young professional hotel-keeper with his mother and father (prematurely-retired bank manager) and they are improving it fast. It has three acres of gardens.

Food & Drink

Until quite recently I could sit cracking lobster claws in the hotel dining room and looking at the boats lowering their lobster pots off Hestan Isle. Alas, lobsters seem to have deserted those beds and now those served come from a few miles along the coast. But Eddie Parker still nets salmon out here and we had one of his catches for dinner last summer, landed that day, served with Balcary sauce of cream and wine with strips of smoked salmon. Sometimes the salmon comes from the lochs and rivers, but it is wild salmon, not farmed. And Eddie's son has a fishing boat and brings in other fresh fish.

With fish so fresh, superb local Galloway beef (which some prize above Angus beef)

produced within a few miles, it is hardly surprising that both the card and the set menu have a heavy 'surf and turf' bias. Even the soups – seafood chowder (seafood soup laced with white wine and cream) and beef consommé (laced with Madeira wine). But there is also a Feather Fowlie (Mary, Queen of Scots' favourite soup – a Scottish cream of chicken with herbs, ham and cream).

You can have haggis for a starter, if you must. You get the traditional dram of whisky with it.

Lobster is served cold with salad, Thermidor (cooked in butter, mustard and parsley, flambéed in brandy, with a cheese sauce), or Hebridean (cooked in butter, mushrooms and cream, flambéed in Drambuie).

The set price menu includes a

starter chosen from the card, followed usually by a roast (lamb, beef or chicken) and a sweet of your choice. Many of the dishes are just as beautifully cooked and fresher than you get in much more expensive places.

The wine list is short, the wines cheap. They have their own 'wine' in Scotland, of which a good 8–15 year old single malt would go well enough with the cheese course but don't drink whisky before or with shellfish. Many who think they had a 'bad' oyster, mussel or even lobster have made this mistake. There is a very reasonably priced Pouilly-Fuissé here to drink with lobster or any fish, a good smokey and fruity Pouilly-Fumé, or one of the very best Muscadets La Galissonnière – a world away from some of the

supermarket Loire battery acids, and one of the best of Sancerre, Clos du Chêne Marchand, back in all its fragrant Sauvignon glory after a bad patch.

I was a little disappointed to find no red really worthy of Galloway beef, but there are good cheap wines. I would go for the highly reputed, dark, powerful Châteauneuf-du-Pape 1979, Chante Cigale of Noël Sabon – a bargain. For something softer, try the 1975 Cissac from Haut Médoc – always reliable.

In fact, for fresh straightforward cooking and reliable inexpensive wines, this hotel is hard to beat.

A smugglers' lair where the beef is superb.

LOCAL DRIVES

Kippford (10m NE), an old fishing village on an estuary, now has a yachting club and an old pub. When the tide is out you can walk to Rough Island, a seabird sanctuary (National Trust for Scotland); an islet is joined to the mainland by a mysterious stone causeway, believed to be a prehistoric path. It was used by smugglers. The Spanish Armada was due to land here in 1588, with help from the Maxwells of Lochmaben Castle, N of Dumfries. Scots Catholics were to join in marching against England. Drake, Hawkins and Howard of Effingham got in the way.

Dumfries (21m NE): Robert Burns came here to live in 1791 as an Exciseman trying to combat smuggling. He wrote here 'Auld Lang Syne' and 'Ye Banks and Braes o'Bonnie Doone'. He died in Mill Vennel (now Burns Street) in 1793. His wife Jean Armour lived in the house until her death in 1834. Now it is a museum. They are buried with several children in St Michael's churchyard and his pew in the kirk is marked with a plaque. He was more often in his 'favourite howff' – Globe Inn, opposite County Hotel, the place to drink his health. Robert Bruce gets a plaque in Castle Street for murdering in 1306 'Red Comyn', the English King's envoy, so launching his fight for Scottish independence, ending in his Bannockburn victory.

Castle Douglas (7m NW) is a pleasant market town. Threave Castle, (2m W of Castle Douglas) is a ruin, once all-powerful; built in the fourteenth century by Archibald the Grim, Earl of Douglas. It was the home of the Black Douglases, who terrorized the Borders, raided constantly into England and had a long feud with English Northumbrian Percy family (Hotspur). Threave Gardens, in the care of the National Trust for Scotland, are open to the public and show the mild climate of this coast, with semi-tropical plants and trees. It is a school for gardeners; pupils take top jobs all over the world.

North-west from Castle Douglas the road to New Galloway runs alongside Loch Ken, a beautiful lake, good for watersports – fishing, sailing, canoeing, waterskiing. Go through New Galloway past Clattering Shaw's Dam, a reservoir made by damming the Dee. A few miles on you may see wild goats on the hillside. Carry on to Newton Stewart, then into the Glentrool and Galloway forests. Here the really magnificent scenery begins – hills, lonely forests, rivers, lakes. See the details in the entry for Knockinaam Lodge, Portpatrick, page 74.

The seascapes southwards are almost as rewarding. Kirkcudbright (pronounced Kirkoobry) has a colony of artists, sculptors and weavers who show their work by the harbour in the art gallery and the sixteenth-century McLellan's Castle, partly restored.

At Gatehouse of Fleet, a fine eighteenth-century town, in the Murray Arms Hotel in 1793, Burns wrote 'March to Bannockburn' which begins 'Scots wha hae wi' Wallace Bled'. Nice forest walks in the grounds of Cally House Hotel. A mile SW is Cardoness Castle, fifteenth-century, well preserved, with fine fireplaces. From Carrick Bay (4m S) at low tide you can walk to Isle of Ardwall. In smuggling days a family called Higgins kept it as a smuggling lair and it is honeycombed with hiding places. Trains of packhorses crossed to Carrick Bay by night.

The Gatehouse–Creetown road was called by Thomas Carlyle 'the finest in the Kingdom'. Creetown has one of the world's best gem rock museums.

Balcraig House by Scone, near Perth, Perthshire, Scotland (take A94 NE from Perth, for 2½m; turning posted to Balcraig on right just before New Scone).
Telephone: Scone (0738) 51123.
DBB D;
SBB B, C.
Dinner D.
Open all year.
No dogs in public rooms.
Credit cards: Euro, Visa, Amex, Diners.

One of our great discoveries among British hotels in ten years. Michael Pearl, barrister, lecturer in law, and Sassenach from Portsmouth, and his wife Kitty took over this solid-looking, neglected Victorian country house in 1981 and have made it one of the greatest country hotels in Scotland. The drawing room and library have comfortable elegance, with well-polished wood, antiques, rich Eastern rugs, fine pictures, authentic crystal chandeliers, a huge leather chesterfield, a fine chaise-longue. Open fires blaze when needed. Bedrooms are all individually designed. I had a huge brass bedstead. You might get an antique four-poster. Bathrooms are modern, efficient and charming, each with hand painted murals on tiles by Scottish artist Sally Anderson. Friendly swans watched me bathe. Some baths are doubles.

The atmosphere, the service, the calm and small thoughtful touches make this a special hotel – like the old-fashioned service of being able to leave your shoes outside the door to be polished overnight. But what makes it very special is its own farm and market garden, run solely to supply its kitchen. There is a herd of pedigree Aberdeen Angus cattle, veal calves in the fields, sheep, goats, pigs, all sorts of poultry, including duck, chicken, geese, gamecock. There is even a herd of wild boar. A hundred types of vegetables are grown, and fifty different herbs, fresh peaches and grapes come from the greenhouse, soft fruits from fields and orchards. The farm is 'free-range' for animals, almost no chemicals are used, and so it is rich in wildlife, from rare birds to rabbits and roe deer.

To work up an appetite, you can play tennis or ride the hotel's Highland ponies ('sturdy and docile'), play golf at the new championship course Murrayshall half a mile away, arrange for salmon fishing on the Tay, trout fishing on a loch, take one of the five-mile walks recommended by the Pearls or play croquet.

Food & Drink

As chef, 23-year-old Eamonn Webster has a big responsibility. With all those delicious, fresh ingredients he would hardly be forgiven if he failed to cook splendid meals. Happily he succeeds, and well deserves the AA rosette. He is not afraid to mix traditional Scottish cooking with modern Continental, nor to invent for himself. I think that we shall hear a lot more of him.

The temptation is to go for something like grilled West Coast langoustines in garlic and herb butter, a vegetable soup, and roast lamb, sirloin of Angus steak or grilled salmon, followed by steamed black treacle pudding with cream from Scone Palace. A true Scottish meal. And why not? But Eamonn offers so many tempting alternatives that the longer you look at the menu, the more indecisive you become.

You could start, as I have done, with deep fried squares of Brie cheese in a salad with strawberry dressing (excellent), or venison terrine with hazelnuts and a purée of onion and Kirsch, or perhaps choux buns filled with creamed avocado and smoked salmon.

I have tried a langoustine and sweetbread soup as the next course, but the cream of courgette and mint soup is a delight, too. Or you can have a sorbet – cider, perhaps, or strawberry and blackcurrant.

For main course, I chose last time venison with port, crème de cassis and poached pear. The venison was tender and flavoursome. Eamonn serves some excellent sauces with ordinary meat and fish, such as a walnut butter sauce with Tay salmon, Armagnac and mustard sauce with sirloin, a delicious nut and herb sauce with lamb.

Vegetables are interesting and tempting. You might try broccoli in herb batter, courgette mousse, tomato stuffed with pineapple, leeks in white wine, baked potato with Stilton, or turnip and heather honey mousse.

Don't eat too much of the excellent savoury dip before starting. Start fairly early and sit as long as you like, because last orders are not until 11p.m. The price includes coffee or tea (a choice of twenty-one teas from Assam or Lapsang Souchong to blackberry or mistletoe).

Michael Pearl really knows about wine and loves it. Before taking to law he worked for his father who catered for banquets, and experience led him to form his own wine company and buy well ahead. 'We only bought the hotel to find room for my wines,' he says, with a poker face. Many wines came from his own personal cellars. The result is a list with superb range, from a nice Brouilly at around £6 to a 1947 Cheval Blanc St Emilion at £137. But whether you buy a 1960 Château Haut Brion, a 1967 Gigondas or a 1979 Domaine de la Renarde white Rully, you are almost certain to pay less than in almost any other good hotel.

I should not worry with the Moniach from Scotland, the red Musar from Lebanon or even the white Great Wall from China (too thin – I have tried it). If you cannot make up your mind, just ask Michael. He adores talking about wine. And whisky. He also has single malts from 115 distillers.

For true lovers –
who also love good wine
and whisky.

LOCAL DRIVES

Scone Palace (2m W – open Easter Saturday to early October), home of the Earls of Mansfield, has fine furniture and porcelain spanning 400 years, old clocks, needlework and superb gardens with rare trees. It was built in 1803 on the site of the old abbey and castle where Scots kings were

crowned from 843. Scotland's Stone of Destiny was here until removed by Edward I to Westminster Abbey.

Perth (3m S), on the beautiful river Tay, was virtual capital of Scotland until 1437, when the Earl of Atholl's men murdered poet-king James I who had reduced the power of the nobles. His widow fled with her son, James II to Edinburgh. The tall spire of St John's Kirk (1243) still soars over the city. Here John Knox, returning from Continental exile, preached the Reformation so effectively that the congregation stoned the high altar, then gutted three monasteries. Visit Huntingtower Castle (2m NW) where Protestant nobles held

James VI for a year to make him change his ministers.

Attractive towns and villages around include Dunkeld (15m NW of Perth) – ruined cathedral in lovely lawns, with fine bridge by Thomas Telford; Crieff (17m W) – overlooking lovely Strathearn; Bridge of Cally (20m N) – attractive village at meeting of rivers, near Glenshee ski slopes.

Pitlochry (28m NW of Perth by A9) is a resort on the river Tummel in a gorgeous setting of loch, river, mountains and woods. It has a Festival theatre.

A 'ladder' helps spawning salmon to climb over the hydro-electric dam, and you

can see them through windows in spring and summer. Along Loch Tummel (B8019) is Queen's View, where Queen Victoria came to see magnificent views of 3,554-ft Schiehallion. North on A9 is the Pass of Killiecrankie (6m) where in 1689 Graham of Claverhouse ('Bonnie Dundee' of Scott's ballad) won a Jacobite victory for James VII over General Mackay but was killed at the moment of victory. Just beyond is Blair Castle of pointed towers and turrets, home of the Duke of Atholl, the only man allowed to keep a private army (open May– mid-October – armour and lovely tapestries).

Banchory Lodge

**Banchory Lodge Hotel
Banchory, Kincardine and
Deeside, Scotland AB3 3HS
(18m from Aberdeen on A93).
Telephone: Banchory (033 02)
2625.
DBB C, D;
SBB B.
Dinner C;
lunch A.
Closed December 10–January
31.
Dogs at management's
discretion.
Credit cards: Euro, Visa,
Amex, Diners.**

Last spring a guest at Banchory Lodge caught a nice big fish in the garden. A 15½-pound salmon, to be precise. To find out why, you don't even have to cross the lawn. From the Regency bow window of one of the two comfortable lounges you can see the salmon jumping high from the waters of the river Dee which passes through the hotel grounds.

The Dee is one of the best salmon rivers in Scotland, and here it meets the smaller but rockier and frothier river Feugh. It is a lovely scene, set off perfectly by the hotel's well-kept lawns and old trees. Even if you never fish you could sit for hours watching the salmon leap, the swallows turning fast but gracefully over the water to catch mosquitoes, gulls flying low to snatch lesser fish, and many rarer birds drinking by the water's edge. Stroll down the long drive to the road and from an eighteenth-century bridge (Brig o'Feugh) you can see salmon rising among the rocks.

It is an informal hotel, run by the Jaffrays since 1966, furnished mostly with Victorian and Edwardian antiques, even the big rooms in the new wing. My bedroom had a huge, carved four-poster bed, a 'day-bed' settee, two armchairs and there was still plenty of room to thrash around. Heavy drapes over the bed and windows were matched. The spacious bathroom was delightful – a green quarter-circle bath in the corner, separate enclosed shower cabin, thick carpet, and everything you need from a good hairdryer to a big rack for clothes drying.

Even the counter of the bar was a fine carved antique from a stately home. Guests return regularly to Banchory Lodge – especially fishermen. The salmon fishing season is February 1 to September 30, but make prior arrangements.

Food & Drink

In a pleasant dining room, the Jaffrays serve meals of traditional British cooking of very good fresh food – apple sauce with the roast pork, bread

sauce and sausage with the roast spring chicken, mint sauce with the leg of lamb, parsley butter with the gorgeous grilled Dee salmon, super fresh sole poached in wine. Very nice, too.

For starters I had one night a ramekin of fresh prawns with cheese sauce, then a real Scottish cock-a-leekie soup made with a good, strong chicken stock. The soups are excellent – made from real old-style stockpots, not squares that you crumble or flavours from packets. My fillet of beef Wellington was real Angus steak. The strawberry meringue pie was light and lovely and the blue Scottish cheese beautifully kept.

American guests in particular seemed delighted with this straightforward cooking.

The wine list, too, is sensible rather than inspired, with many wines under £7 (1985), enough medium-priced wines to give you a little choice in each area, and three fine red wines for celebrations – a 1970 Château Brane Cantenac, the second-growth Margaux which I love enough to buy ahead to age, a real first-growth Château Latour, one of the greatest wines in the world, from Pauil-lac, a 1967 at a price much cheaper than in most restaurants or hotels. And a 1977 Gevrey-Chambertin Champonnets, one of the best of the first growths of this delightful red Burgundy.

The Muscadet is also one of the very best (la Galissonière) and is a pound or two cheaper than on most lists. Just the wine to drink with Dee salmon.

The freshest salmon in Scotland

The North Sea oil boom-town of Aberdeen, still also a fishing port, is eighteen miles NE. The fish market comes to life around 4a.m., with sales starting at 7a.m. North of Aberdeen are Balmedie sands, a ten-mile straight sand beach backed by dunes, with safe swimming most of the year.

Crathes Castle (3m E of Banchory on A93) is a sixteenth-century baronial hall, with an Elizabethan fireplace in the Great Hall and an ivory horn which belonged to Robert Bruce. Haunted room with painted ceiling. The eighteenth-century garden has some of Britain's finest plant collections, including a lovely Pool Garden (open Easter and May 1–September 30).

Drum Castle (8m NE) – the keep was built by King Robert Bruce in 1280. He gave it to the Irvines, who still own it. You can see fine silver, furniture and old Masters.

A93 westwards from Banchory follows Royal Deeside to Aboyne, historic castle of the Gordons; at Lumphanan, 5m NW of Aboyne, cairn where King Macbeth lost to Malcolm and died in 1057; Ballater, a busy resort surrounded by lovely wooded hills, with 3,786-ft Lochnagar rising to the SW; Birkhall, an early eighteenth-century house, was bought by Edward VII and is now used by the Queen Mother; Balmoral Castle (32m from Banchory at Crathie) – bought by Queen Victoria and Albert in 1853, still used by the Royal family. Grounds only open May–July when family are not there. Crathie Church is where they worship; Braemar (6m on), scene in September of Royal Highland Gathering, which the Queen usually attends. N of Banchory by A980 is another drive with fine scenery to Alford (Craigievar – fairytale castle unchanged since it was built in 1626).

Billesley Manor

Billesley Manor Hotel Billesley, Nr Stratford-upon-Avon, Warwickshire B49 6NF (just off A422 about halfway between Stratford and Alcester).
Telephone: (0789) 763737.
DBB D;
SBB B.
Dinner D.
Open all year.
Credit cards: Euro, Visa, Amex, Diners.

William Shakespeare warmed his pantaloons before the big log fire under the oak panels and crest of Sir Robert Lee, sometime Lord Mayor of London. So can we. Shakespeare had free use of Sir Robert's library. In my fine Elizabethan bedroom I had to make do with two mediocre novels and the Bible. No doubt he could have made a play from them. I didn't write a line. But I did have an electric trouser-press – useless for pantaloons.

I like this handsome manor not only as a beautiful historic house in eleven acres of pleasant garden and parkland but as a peaceful, elegant hideout for exploring Stratford and Warwick, then retreating from the crowds. But it is by no means dead or sombre.

It belonged to the Trussel family of warrior lords from 1066–1592, when Lee 'modernized' it, adding a stone front. More recently it was a country club, and a few souvenirs of that period remain, including an excellent indoor swimming pool and an ostentatiously-grand modern bathroom with gold fitments, seemingly made for a TV soap ad but attached to a grand Elizabethan bedroom with huge four-poster and a priest's hole. The hidden priest could survey the bed through a peep-hole in the panelling. A preview of someone's confession!

My room overlooked old gardens and modern yew topiary of trees cut to form heads of a mouse, poodle, hedgehog, rabbit and fox. Others look across lawns and an old stone lily-pond to the long drive and main gates. Some locks and door-fittings have an armourer's mark of 1600.

One of the two pleasant dining rooms was the Elizabethan kitchen, and it still has a huge chimney-place where you can imagine oxen roasting on spits and hams being smoked.

Shakespeare himself retreated here from Stratford.

Graffiti.

Food & Drink

Ian David Whittock, who came from the Waldorf, has in a short time earned Billesley Manor a deserved AA rosette for cooking. He is very inventive but not deliberately seeking to shock traditionalists. His set menus (not cheap) are nicely balanced and good value. Last time I was there you could have fried chicken breasts with a touch of garlic and spring onion on salad as a starter, then scallops in pastry with tomato and basil butter, a sorbet (super, but too small), lamb cutlets with a lovely grain mustard sauce, and a magnificent hot strawberry omelette in raspberry sauce. His desserts are truly outstanding. I defy the most ardent slimmer to pass them by. Try, for instance, Timbale Amelia – a biscuit filled with freshly-poached peach, apricot and ice cream on a bed of raspberry sauce covered with spun sugar!

Moving to dearer choices from the card, you find smoked chicken salad with asparagus and mustard vinaigrette; sliced turbot in pastry with chive sauce; chicken mousse filled with Stilton cheese, Armagnac and walnuts, poached and served with cream of fresh herb sauce on a bed of apple. Those are just starters. A favourite main course is loin of lamb cooked in butter, coated with mint-flavoured soufflé and served with port wine sauce. Gorgeous!

Such dishes deserve excellent wines and there are plenty on the list for those who can afford them. It is a mouth-watering list, but I did find the prices a little too high, even for house-wines. Some of the clarets are good choices, and the Rhône Coteaux du Tricastin 1981 was good value and would go well with the lamb cutlets with mustard sauce. But it would be worth paying extra for the 1979 Château Les Ormes Sorbet

these days to the famous Brolio of Barone Ricasoli.

An interesting wine is the 1981 red Rully from Côte Chalonaise, where white wines normally predominate. This one, a fruity, balanced wine, is from Domaine de la Renarde of Jean-François Delorme, who has performed near-miracles in improving the wines of this area. The reds here are definitely earthier than the delicate whites.

For my white wine, with the smoked chicken, I chose a 1982 Saumur from Jacques Collé's Château de Parnay. Still Saumur white wines have improved greatly and this is one of the best.

from Médoc. There is also the well-known Marquès de Riscal Rioja from Spain, called 1980, but Spanish blending allows wines of different years to be mixed. Perhaps the best bargain on the list and very good for accompanying Ian Whittock's richer sauces is the Antinori Chianti Classico. I find wine produced by Marchese Antinori to be at least equal

There are some super vintage ports to go with Ian Whittock's good selection of cheeses, and a very palatable Edward Sheldon 1981 crusted port – much cheaper.

Stratford (4m E) is inevitably crowded with sightseers but keeps its beauty. Of Shakespeare (born here in 1564) you can still see his likely birthplace in Henley Street, the schoolroom in the Guildhall where he learned his first lessons, an Elizabethan knot garden near the foundations of New Place, where he died, his tomb in Holy Trinity church, the glorious gabled Tudor house where his daughter Susanna and her husband lived, and his wife Anne Hathaway's cottage, thatched and timbered, at Shottery. The Birthplace Trust in Henley Street has a museum, library and information. His plays are

performed by players worthy of him at the Royal Shakespeare Theatre and at the newer theatre, The Other Place, associated with it.

Stratford is still a market town and is rich in lovely river scenes and superb buildings, including a Palladian town hall (1767), the fifteenth-century Falcon inn, and Harvard House, built in 1596 by the father of Katherine Rogers. She married Robert Harvard of Southwark and their son founded Harvard University, USA.

Stratford also has a collection of vintage and veteran cars.

Charlecote Park (4m E of Stratford) has been the home

of the Lucy family since 1558. They still live there, but the National Trust owns it and you can visit at set times. Its deer park, with fallow and red deer, is where Shakespeare was arrested for poaching. The house has superb furniture and paintings.

Alcester (4m W of Billesley) nice small town where the Arrow and the Alne rivers meet. See narrow Butter Street with ancient roofs, seventeenth-century bayed Churchill House, the Priory with an odd Victorian neo-Gothic folly, 1618 town hall.

Warwick (8m NE of Stratford) has one of the greatest castles in Europe (see Regent Hotel, Leamington Spa, page 134).

Bishopstrow House

**Bishopstrow House
Boreham Road, Warminster,
Wiltshire BA12 9HH (2m SE on
A36).
Telephone: (0985) 212312.
SBB C;
DBB C, D (Continental
breakfast – English breakfast
extra).
Dinner menu D (three
courses); D+ (four courses).
Lunch menu C.
Always open.
Euro, Visa, Amex.**

This handsome, gracious late Georgian mansion in a 27-acre park is furnished with such flair and taste and run with such willing, friendly and efficient service that it is one of a handful of British hotels admitted to the French Relais et Châteaux group, is given a rating of 84 per cent by Egon Ronay (the sixth highest mark in England outside London) and has three red stars from the AA. Furthermore, the AA gives it a coveted rosette for cooking and Ronay calls its cooking 'excellent' and praises restaurant service and comfort. I can only add my own accolade for the delightful hotel which Kurt Schiller and his retiring wife have made from a beautiful but run-down private house. I love it.

From a comfortable entrance hall you can enter an elegant morning room, with antique furnishings and oil paintings – the sort of room where it would be a pleasure to be kept waiting, and a delightful, comfortable lounge with curved bay windows and a log fire when it is needed. The quality of everything, from furniture to carpets and rugs, is a delight. Flower arrangements are

beautiful. The same quality and good taste continue in the bedrooms, most of which are furnished with antiques but some in tasteful modern style. I had a lovely large room with views over the driveway, lawns and wooded park to the Doric temple and summerhouse in the grounds. Curtains and bedspreads matched and the bathroom was beautifully finished with Italian tiles. It provided all my needs, plus scales, which I hid, so as not to spoil my dinner. There was colour TV and flowers and fruit in the bedroom.

In a former stable block attached to the house, an interior designer was putting finishing touches to some charming new modern rooms which will now be ready.

Next to the outdoor heated swimming pool, pleasantly set among columns and arches so that you might expect an ancient Greek beauty to slip out of her clothes and into the water, they were also building an indoor pool in the same style. It has a sauna and solarium. There are outdoor and indoor tennis courts.

The grounds are very pleasant – tended but not too formal. There is an ancient burial mound and a tumulus as well as the Doric temple. The river Wylye flows alongside, with trout fishing in season.

Food & Drink

Young Simon Collins cooked with Robert Carrier at Hintlesham Hall until that superb restaurant closed. Then Kurt Schiller invited him to Bishopstrow House. Everyone I know is glad that he stayed.

He cooks with a light modern touch, but is not slavishly attached to modern French fashions. His most famous dish is a roulade of chicken (chicken breast filled with spinach and served with a Marsala sauce), but I like just as much his chicken breasts in a Calvados sauce with glazed apple. He also makes a really delicious blackcurrant sauce which he serves with several dishes, including thinly-sliced calves' liver. It goes superbly with rack of venison. Another of his inventive dishes is pork fillet, coated with crushed almonds, cooked in butter and served with a mango sauce.

His best known starter is thin slices of monkfish and trout marinated in fresh lime juice with coriander and ginger. I was a little dubious because I think that the Chinese use ginger in cooking better than Europeans, but this was delicious. He makes a very light and creamy terrine of sole and salmon, served with a tomato sauce.

I think the four-course meals are worth the extra cost because his middle courses are inventive and very interesting. His courgette soufflé is a tomato filled with courgette soufflé and a courgette filled with tomato sorbet; the sorbet is especially nice. Another dish is brill fillet, lightly cooked, wrapped in spinach and served in a pastry case with a red wine sauce. I may be wrong, but that seems to have more than a touch of Robert Carrier about it. Vegetables are excellently cooked, desserts superb.

The dining room is attractive, with a little conservatory attached for summer eating. The plates shine, the cutlery glistens, the food is attractively presented and the service is very friendly but professional.

Your first glance at the wine list might turn you pale. Second item is a Château Petrus Pomerol 1947 for £425, and there is nothing on the first page cheaper than a 1957 Lafite Rothschild at £85!

On the second page is a fine selection of vintage clarets from around £15. Lynch Moussas 1979 Pauillac which would go well with the roulade of chicken. There is also a 1970 La Lagune, a good year of a wine I have always liked very much, in a magnum at £75. I asked who drank this. A famous photographer of the very old school and a more famous peer always split a magnum when they dine here, it seems. Why didn't I become a photographer?

The red Burgundy list is almost as exciting. The strong flavoured, rich minerally Echézeaux would go well with the liver or venison. To get down to earth, the housewines are a most drinkable red Burgundy at £7.50 and a white Bordeaux.

There is a full, fruity Brouilly from Beaujolais shipped by the commendable Boisset. If you love good white Burgundy as much as I do, you won't mind paying for Marcel Vincent's Château Fuissé. It would go so well with Simon Collins' starters and second course. But I also recommend the '82 Sancerre from a small producer. It is exceptionally good.

Whatever you choose, Simon Collins' cooking deserves good wine. We shall hear a lot more of him.

LOCAL DRIVES

Warminster (2m) is an old market town now cursed by lorry traffic, but it still has old market inns. St Lawrence church was founded in the thirteenth century, closed by Edward VI, and bought back by the townsfolk in 1675 for £38 6s 8d. This is Salisbury Plain and Army camps abound. Just outside Westbury (3m N of Warminster) on Bratton Down is cut in the hillside the oldest of Wiltshire's several white horses. Believed to have commemorated King Alfred's victory over the Danes in the ninth century, it was originally more like a carthorse until a steward to Lord Abingdon (named Gee) recut it to look 'more elegant' in 1778. It is 180ft long. Chalcot House (2m SW Westbury) is a small seventeenth-century Palladian manor with a grandiose Victorian porch; inside are mementoes of the Indian Raj, the Boer War, the Victorian reign and a collection of modern paintings.

Longleat House (5m SW of Warminster) is a wonderful showpiece. One of the most beautiful Elizabethan houses left, it was completed in 1580 for Sir John Thynne at a cost of just over £8,000 and is the home of his descendant, the Marquess of Bath, who was one of the first to open his stately home to the public. The inside is magnificent and historically interesting. The Italian styled State rooms are breath-taking. The gardens and park, laid out by Capability Brown, most famous of landscape gardeners, in the eighteenth century, are still superb. (He was called 'Capability' because, when asked if a site were suitable for gardens or a park, he would answer: 'It has Capability'). A half-mile walk through woodlands coloured in June with azaleas and rhododendrons leads to Heaven's Gate on the Warminster road, with superb views of the grounds and house 400ft below in the valley.

The grounds are best known these days for the Safari Park, where wild animals include lions, cheetahs, giraffes.

Shaftesbury area (16m S) – see Plumber Manor Hotel (see page 121). Bath (19m NW) – see Homewood Park Hotel (see page 62).

Stonehenge (18m E) – the awesome and mysterious group of raised stones brought here around 1800–1400BC – is believed to have been the site of religious sun worship. Bluestones were brought 200 miles from Pembrokeshire in South Wales, probably floated across the Bristol Channel on rafts, then dragged over tracks of logs.

Salisbury (21m SE) is a truly lovely cathedral city, at the meeting place of four river valleys in a fold of the hills. The lovely cathedral spire dominates the town, which was founded in 1220 when a bishop abandoned the nearby Norman cathedral at Old Sarum hill fort because it lacked water. The present edifice was finished in 1258 but the spire was added in 1334. It is 404 feet high and the highest in England. The cathedral is pure Early English Gothic and one of the loveliest in Europe. Inside, it is spacious with dramatic Purbeck stone columns, interesting tombs and monuments and a dialless clock from 1326. The Cathedral Close has thirteenth-century houses, with two museums, and mediaeval streets of half-timbered houses and over-hanging upper floors lead to the market place.
(See also Lainston House Hotel, page 77.)

One of Britains very best county hotels.

**Bodysgallen Hall Hotel
Llandudno,
Gwynedd,
North Wales
LL30 1RS
(just off B5115 road S from
Llandudno).
Telephone: Llandudno (0492)
84466.
DBB C–E;
SBB B–C.
Dinner C;
lunch A.
Closed one week in February.
Credit cards: Euro, Visa,
Amex, Diners.**

This dignified old house, whose building spread over 600 years from the thirteenth century, was the first to be restored and made into an hotel by Historic House Hotels. Small wonder that it has won them the Prince of Wales and Europa Nostra awards for restoration of an historic building, and that it is the only hotel in Wales to have the much-coveted three red stars from the AA. It is a harmonious, elegant, supremely comfortable masterpiece which sends some travellers into raptures.

It is set on a ridge in the hills south of Llandudno and although wings were still added as late as 1905, it makes a harmonious whole, almost uniform. There are views to Conwy Castle and glimpses of mountains in the Snowdonia National Park from its 40-acre park, of which seven acres are lovely cultivated gardens. You will love the walled rose garden, lily pond, rockery with a cascade and a rare and intricate seventeenth-century knot garden of box hedges filled with sweet scented herbs.

Inside the whole house has been lovingly restored, decorated and furnished. Directly you walk into the oak-panelled hall you catch the spirit of the house – big stone fireplace, stone mullioned windows but great comfortable settees and armchairs to entice relaxation. The lovely oak-panelled drawing room above it, with huge windows, has the same atmosphere of age-old comfort, with a stone fireplace surrounded by old Delft tiles, overmantle with arms of previous owners, the Wynns and the Vaughans, sink-in seats and big bay window.

Bedrooms above are all different, mainly large, some with four-poster beds, all with fine bathrooms with heavy brass fittings. A stone spiral staircase leads up to a thirteenth-century tower with fine views of Conwy Castle below, looking like a model.

Around a flowery courtyard in the grounds are cottages converted into peaceful suites with bedrooms and lounge. They do some interesting winter theme weekends – wine, gourmet, gardens.

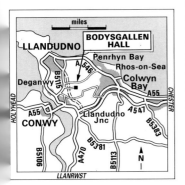

Food & Drink

Chef David Harding has to please three people – those who like traditional cooking, those looking constantly for something different and the Welsh, who are a tiny bit nationalistic about ingredients. To them Welsh lamb is the best in the world. So is Carmarthen ham, Welsh trout, Welsh salmon and Welsh duck, not to mention leeks.

Luckily he uses these splendid ingredients, even locally-smoked salmon, and uses them well. He does admit that his steak comes from Scotland.

On the set-price menu last time Barbara chose a really pleasant spinach and apple soup with cream. Then came the Welsh lamb. It was sautéed in red wine, and was delicious. Not a Welshman cried: 'Sacrilege', though I confess that I would just as soon have his rack of lamb roasted with ginger, rosemary, honey and cider. That was on the card.

For dessert Barbara had a honey and walnut mousse, of which she heartily approved. Most diners went for fresh plum tart with cream. We are rarely offered old-style fruit tarts these days. They are mixed with strawberry vinegar or kiwi fruit or avocado or mint or something. Cheese was a separate course and there was a fair selection of British and French with celery. There were three choices on each course and the meal was good value.

But Welsh salt duck is David Harding's speciality and I am looking forward to trying it. And his fresh crab tart. Even his gin and tonic sorbet, though Champagne has always seemed a better drink to me.

The kitchen supplies good picnics for all-day explorers.

The dining room is light, uncluttered, charmingly decorated and has a square bay window with most pleasant views. The wine list is worthy of this delightful old house, with a very palatable cheap house claret, some fairly sensible prices for nearly-great wines, like a 1967 Lynches Bages, a 1971 Talbot and a 1969 Moreau Nuits-St-Georges Burgundy. But for the Lamb or almost any main course I would pick the 1967 Château Haut-Brion at a most reasonable price for a Premier Cru wine. Not an 'expert's' year I admit, but excellent at this price. I hope that they save some for me.

There are two good Italian wines at lower than usual prices, too – a 1979 Barolo and Classico Chianti 1978 from Villa Antinori. Try this with lamb. Chianti is made under much stricter controls than most wines of Europe and the good Classico and Classico Riserva wines are some of the best value in Europe.

Barbara found among the end of bin wines a 1982 St Véran white Burgundy which pleased her.

There is even a Welsh wine listed, called Croffta, produced so rightly, by a Mr Bevan. But the Pride of Bodysgallen is the list of Château Gruard-Larose from St Julien. With my annual intake and love of St Julien, I do not know how I have missed this one. Especially as it is a Cordier property, like my beloved Talbot, and also produced in large oak vats which make for good wine even in a mediocre year like 1967. I am told that the wines are heavier than Talbot, that they are all smooth and fruity, that the 1977 is charming, the 1976 rich, the 1970 is deliciously fruity, the 1967 is one of the best of that mediocre year and that 1961 is superlative. It is also very expensive. The 1975 has 'style'. That's for me.

The best hotel in Wales.

The hotel will give you a pamphlet with map of thirty-seven interesting places to visit. The resort of Llandudno, on a headland with beaches pointing two ways, is 2m N; plenty of summer entertainment. Conwy (2m S) is a most attractive mediaeval town with a well-preserved and dramatic thirteenth-century castle and town walls built by Edward I of England to keep the Welsh in Wales. Three bridges over the Conway river include Telford's beautiful suspension bridge of 1826.

At Bodnant (5m S) is one of Britain's finest gardens – seventy acres sloping to the Conway river with Snowdonia as a backcloth. Laid out in 1875, it is known for magnolias, azaleas, rhododendrons and cypressus (National Trust).

St Asaph (18m E) is a walled village-city, with one of the smallest cathedrals in Britain, founded 573AD; the building is partly Norman, mostly fifteenth century. Following the A55 west along the coast (from Llandudno) at the top of the Snowdonia National Park, you find the spectacular waterfalls of Aber, near Llanfairfechan, then Penrhyn Castle, in pure Norman style but built 1820–45. Further on is Bangor, where the Telford suspension bridge built in 1826 connects with the Isle of Anglesey. Fairly horrific traffic jams can still happen near here in midsummer or during peak business hours, despite a new bypass.

Over on Anglesey is the Marquis of Anglesey's fine seaside house and gardens designed by James Wyatt – Plas Newydd (National Trust owned; the present Marquess lives in part of it, the rest is open to the public).

Past Bangor on the mainland is Caernarfon Castle, thirteenth century, very beautiful, where the first Prince of Wales, son of Edward I, was born in 1284 and where Prince Charles was invested Prince of Wales in 1969. Inland four miles is Bryn Bras Castle, a romantic castle with fine gardens.

Inland eight miles is Llanberis, the rugged Llanberis Pass and the mountain railway that leads to the top of Snowdon (3,650ft – 2½ hours with ½ hour at the peak). It is a glorious mountain but if you intend to climb it on foot get all information on routes, weather and clothing, whatever anyone else is doing.

The Snowdonia National park covers 840 square miles of spectacular and lovely mountains, forests, lakes and estuaries, with twenty-five miles of coast.

For more information on the Snowdonia National Park, Blaenau Ffestiniog steam railway and other sights, see Palé Hall Hotel, Bala, page 111, and Porth Tocyn Hotel, Abersoch, page 124.

Breamish House

**Breamish House Hotel
Powburn, Alnwick,
Northumberland NE66 4LL
(leave A1 just N of Morpeth,
take A697 to Powburn
village).
Telephone: Powburn (066
578) 266.
DBB B;
SBB A.
Dinner B;
lunch A.
Closed January.
No credit cards.**

Take someone who prefers wildlife to a wild life. Pack walking shoes and a good book on feathered birds. Otters hunt the Pow Burn which runs through the garden of this elegant Victorian village house made from an original Tudor hunting lodge. Trout abound in the river Breamish 400 yards away. Badgers come to the water at dusk. In half an hour I have seen spotted fly catchers, tree creepers, tree linnets and a heron, all within the five-acre garden and woods. Owls hoot at night. There is a bird research station down the road at Glanton. Sheep, goats and horses peer at you over the garden fence and rabbits play in thousands in the next meadow.

Graham Taylor, who ran a successful hotel in Gateshead, has performed miracles here in three years. Already Breamish House has two coveted AA red stars and a rosette for cooking. It is a friendly, intimate country house rather than an hotel.

The large sitting room has a touch of Victorianism, with white colonnaded book cases, wing chairs and a huge settee in green velvet, but it is not cluttered. Nor is the dining room, where the tables are all of old, polished wood in different shapes.

Most bedrooms are large, airy, comfortable, with good-sized bathrooms. Iced water in a thermos and a tin of homemade biscuits are provided in each as well as a huge teamaker which has radio, buzzer, flasher, teamaker. I was glad of the colour TV to see England beat Australia.

Graham admits to a difficulty in finding good staff in such a remote spot. As soon as he trains them, they disappear to the bright lights of the seaside or Newcastle. But those he has cope very well, including the mathematics master who is part-time waiter. He could, I feel, get a job as a Maître d'Hôtel.

You may meet more animals than people!

Food & Drink

Graham Taylor is too modest about his hotel's cooking. 'Nothing particularly outstanding, but varied and reasonably priced,' he says. Well, the AA do not throw away red rosettes, and I have found the cooking fairly straightforward, very good and excellent value.

At my last dinner there the starters included egg and prawns with curried mayonnaise, the well-liked Breamish paté (pork, liver, chicken with pine kernels) and an avocado and green pepper paté, which was delicious.

The soup of watercress, sorrel and almond was delicate, with a very subtle blend of flavours.

From four main courses I chose roast loin of English lamb with apricot and celery stuffing and a tart mint jelly, and I wish I knew how to make that stuffing. Definitely more subtle than it sounds. Plenty of good, fresh vegetables, mostly from the hotel garden.

From the sweets I chose ginger syllabub in a brandy snap case. Cheese and coffee were included in the modest price. Even the rolls were home-made. For breakfast I had *two* of those superb Craster kippers.

The 76 wines on the list included a dozen varied half bottles. All were very modestly priced. There were no great wines. The best was a fifth-growth 1979 Pauillac from Bordeaux at around £12 for a full bottle (1985). I had a pleasant Muscadet and a pretty good Chianti Classico Reserva 1979 (not up to Antinori standards, but by no means to be despised) and both cost under £5 a bottle. This list has one of the lowest mark-ups I have experienced at a good hotel.

There are nine well-chosen German white wines, all except one medium to medium sweet. A lot of people come here to dine from as far away as Newcastle, and these are the wines most of them choose.

Breamish House will not send you away bankrupt.

Many guests forget their cars and take to their feet for a week. This is on the edge of the magnificent Cheviots and the Northumberland National Park, stretching to the Scottish Borders, and is one of the wildest and least crowded areas of Britain, little known to most of us. The coast is undiscovered, too – little visited and unspoiled. North from Alnwick it is designated as an Area of Outstanding Natural Beauty. One of the few places known at all is Craster, 6m NE from Alnwick – famous for its kippers and salmon smoked in sheds above the harbour. It also has wonderful cliff scenery. Explore this area along little roads. Take these SW to Alnwick (10m), historic and attractive town, with ruins of the Percy's twelfth-century castle (early British and Roman antiquities in the Postern Tower).

Alnmouth, once a grain port, is now a yachtsman's holiday centre. Past Craster N (1m on foot) are the ruins of fourteenth-century Dunstanburgh Castle, brooding impressively on a great rock jutting into the sea, as Turner painted it. There follows a series of rocks, sand beaches and dunes with fishermen's cottages and some holiday villas. Little harbours at Beadnell, and Seahouses with boats in calm weather to Farne Islands, rocky islets sheltering many species of seabirds and grey seals. St Cuthbert lived alone here and returned to die.

Bamburgh has a huge Norman castle, once seat of the Kings of Northumbria, almost completely restored. In the graveyard of the thirteenth-century church is buried Grace Darling, born in

the unspoilt fishing village in 1815. She became a national heroine in 1838 when she rowed with her father from a lighthouse in a raging gale to rescue wrecked sailors.

Ros Castle, twelve miles NE of Powburn, has superb views from the 1,036ft hill. Nearby Chillingham Castle grounds have a rare breed of wild white cattle, descendants of wild

oxen trapped here in 1220.

For sights South of Alnwick and others, see Linden Hall Hotel, Longhorsley, Morpeth, page 87.

BURLEIGH COURT

Burleigh Court Hotel
Minchinhampton, Nr Stroud,
Gloucestershire GL5 2PF
(2½m SE of Stroud off A419
Stroud–Cirencester road).
Telephone: Brimscombe
(0453) 883804.
DBB C;
SBB B.
Dinner B;
lunch A.
Closed December 24–31.
Dogs by arrangement.
Credit cards: Euro, Visa,
Amex.

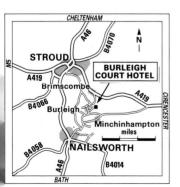

I am *so* glad that I found Burleigh Court. It does not have quite the polish and elegance of some of my favourites but you cannot beat it for friendliness and hospitality.

I cannot think of it as an hotel. There is no reception desk, but very warm handshakes. Most of the guests seem to be old friends of the Benson family from previous visits. You don't see many hotelkeepers spending their coffee-break in front of the fire with guests, doing the *Telegraph* crossword, as Roger Benson does, or popping out of the kitchen to weed a flower-bed, as Hilary does. As for the 'barmaid, waitress and bag-carrier', daughter Jo – the lights must have dimmed in the computer engineering industry when she abandoned it to bring her smile home to Burleigh. Sadly, another daughter who was a trained chef died quite recently, but her former assistant is keeping up her standards.

The 200-year-old Cotswold-stone house looks across old lawns, trees and a lily pond, over a few houses to a hillside of trees and sheep. I was as concerned as Roger when badgers tore up the old lawn one night. But he said: 'I would never drive out badgers.' The back terrace, where you can eat on fine days, looks up to lawns, flower beds and a stone Victorian 'plunge pool' – deep, small and heated. The grounds cover five acres, and were laid out originally by Sir Clough Williams-Ellis, who created the showpiece village of Portmeirion in Wales.

Bedrooms are very comfortable, bright and cheerful, befitting a friendly country house.

The bar is big and has log fires in colder weather, the lounge more intimate.

Food & Drink

I love traditional sauces, really well made, and that is what you find at Burleigh Court. You can often get a fine steak and kidney pudding, too.

There is a good choice on each course. That leaves me with problems, like whether to go for the superb cream of Stilton

Dishes are fresh and vary according to season. In winter you might be offered as a main course choice a roast guinea fowl with a butter of juniper berries, thyme, onion and lemon or pillows of chicken (chicken breasts poached in wine, topped with mushrooms in Madeira sauce and baked in puff pastry – very nice). There is always an old-fashioned dish like steak and kidney, lamb stew or roast leg of lamb marinaded in mustard sauce. They serve a Slimmer's Dish, too. Last time I was there it was a very aromatic devilled turkey – marinaded in mustard, tabasco, Worcestershire sauce and lemon juice and served in a pepper sauce! There is also a vegetarian dish. I suspect Jo is partly responsible, being a vegetarian herself.

The sweet trolley is magnificent – worthy of any gastronomic grand restaurant, and no good for slimmers at all.

The meals are excellent value. So are the wines – a fairly short list, not very ambitious and easy on the pocket. Apart from Champagne, the dearest in 1985 was a 1982 Gevrey-Chambertin at £11.45. The Valpolicella, taken young in Italy and lapped in litres, was £3.75 a bottle.

For German wine lovers, there is a Riesling 1982 from Eitelsbacher, where the little river Ruwer meets the Moselle, at £6.75. It is a 'Spätlese', from late-picked grapes, and therefore has a full flavour. As an aperitif I would choose the Muscadet-sur-Lie at £4.75. Leaving the wine longer on the lees and bottling it direct does not impress some wine-lovers

soup or the light and lovely salmon éclairs – little boats of choux pastry filled with fresh salmon mousse, served with a delicious cucumber sauce (one of the best I have tasted). The deep fried cheese crêpes are delicious, too, and the scallops are served with a sauce of mushroom, tomato and cheese.

but it gives a much fruitier flavour. For my starters I chose the Premier Cru Chablis Vaillon, a favourite of mine and for the steak and kidney pudding or guinea fowl there is a choice of three Château bottled 1978–9 clarets at low ·prices. The Médoc Brie-Caillou is exceptional for a Bourgeois wine.

Neither eating nor wine-bibbing at Burleigh Court will break the bank.

Glorious hill country all round, though Stroud, the old wool town on a steep hill, has lost much of its charm through modernization but has at Lansdown an interesting museum of wool and weaving.

Minchinhampton, a mile from Burleigh, has a 600-acre common belonging to the National Trust with fine views over the Golden Valley and Stroudwater Hills. The village was once given by Matilda, wife of William the Conqueror, to the newly-founded Abbaye-aux-Dames in Caen, Normandy. The old village church has a fine pinnacled tower.

Badminton House (13m S off A46 – Great Badminton) is a superb Palladian mansion remodelled by William Kent in 1740 from a 1682 house. The Dukes of Beaufort have lived here for 300 years and the estate still covers 52,000 acres. The house has a collection of English, Italian and Dutch paintings and much fine carving by Grinling Gibbons. You can also see the kennels and stables of the Beaufort Hunt. The house is closed for

re-decoration but is due to re-open sometime in 1986. The Great Badminton Three Day Event Horse Trials are held in spring, usually attended by the Royal Family. Doddington House and carriage museum are three miles to the south-east (see Homewood Park).

Horton Court (15m SW of Minchinhampton – just off A46; 3m NE of Chipping Sodbury) fourteenth–fifteenth century gabled manor house in Cotswold stone, same period church, and twelfth-century hall. The hall, altered over centuries, is still a link between Saxon and mediaeval halls. Garden includes huge tulip tree (Hall and garden open April–October; Wednesday and Saturday p.m. National Trust.)

Chipping Sodbury (18m SW Minchinhampton on A432 just off A46 is a little market town; typical Cotswold wide main street with Georgian brick and Cotswold stone buildings. Fifteenth century church of St John the Baptist restored 1869 by Street who designed London's Law Courts. He rediscovered interesting pulpit – canopied, and reached by a hole in a pillar.

Slimbridge Wild Fowl Trust (on river Severn 12m W of Burleigh Court) was founded by artist and ornithologist Sir Peter Scott (son of explorer Scott of the Antarctic) in 1946. It has the biggest and most varied collection of waterfowl in the world. Swans, geese, ducks, flamingos and other birds can be seen in natural surroundings. 5,000 wild geese winter in the estuary. You can watch them from

towers. Just south of Slimbridge is Berkeley, charming Georgian town known now for Double Gloucester cheese and a nuclear power station. The Fitzhardings, Earls of Berkeley have lived in the castle since the twelfth century. In 1327 King Edward II was murdered in the dungeon at the request of his wife and Earl Mortimer. In the mediaeval Berkeley church is the grave of Edward Jenner, discoverer of vaccination, who died in 1823, and memorial windows to him showing Christ healing the sick.

Within fifteen miles of Burleigh Court are three fascinating towns – Cirencester (market town with lovely walks in 3,000 acre park); Gloucester (industrial city, historic, one of the four major Roman colonies in Britain; inland port. The cathedral, started in 1089, with later additions through centuries, is the best illustration of architectural changes in Europe. One magnificently coloured window celebrating the English victory at Crécy in 1346 is 72ft by 38ft, second largest mediaeval stained glass window after York Minster's; Cheltenham (one of Europe's finest spas) with Regency houses, crescents and squares to rival Bath. Its Music Festival is one of our greatest.

You'll soon be one of the family here!

CAVENDISH HOTEL

Cavendish Hotel
Baslow, Derbyshire DE4 1SP
(in Chatsworth Park: on A619
at Baslow village).
Telephone: Baslow (024688)
2311.
DBB D;
SBB (no single rooms) C.
Dinner (card) C–D.
Open all year.
Credit cards: Visa, Amex,
Diners.

Sit back in the armchair beside your bedroom window in this gracious hotel looking across the beautiful Chatsworth estate and dream that you are a Duke or Duchess. The Cavendish is in the grounds of the Duke of Devonshire's Chatsworth Park, and although you cannot see his house, the stateliest of homes, you can walk across to visit it.

There has been an inn here for centuries, and by the eighteenth century it was a famous fishing inn called the Peacock. In 1975 the present Duchess of Devonshire restored it, giving it twenty-three luxury bedrooms. In 1984 ten extra bedrooms were added, using the same local stone as the original. The Duchess took charge of the décor and furnishing and it is all in comfortable good taste with a lived-in look. Some of the antique furniture and most of the pictures came from Chatsworth House, and the fitments for the new rooms were made in the estate carpenter's shop which she supervises.

Barbara took a long time to get to bed. She was admiring the fascinating paintings, old prints and photographs on the corridor walls.

Eric Marsh, a young highly-trained professional, leases the hotel from the Duke and Duchess and runs it immaculately.

The Duke's family name is Cavendish. One of his ancestors founded the Cavendish Laboratory at Cambridge University. Another was Prime Minister. The Duchess is one of the Mitford sisters (Deborah), best known of whom are the writer Nancy, Jessica, involved in anti-Fascist politics, and Unity, who was involved with Hitler. The new bedrooms are named after them. Ours was Lucy – interesting and comfortable, with two windows overlooking the park, two armchairs and such niceties as brown bath robes, two reproductions of court masques by Inigo Jones from the Devonshire collection, and a presentation box of 'forget-tables', including toothbrush and shampoo.

One of the three lounges is so

comfortable it is difficult to leave it — even to go into the bar. A quietly alluring hotel.

The hotel has been famous for trout fishing for 150 years and fly fishing is available on ten miles of Chatsworth's rivers, the Derwent and Wye.

Food & Drink

The joy of eating here is the game from Chatsworth Park, beautifully cooked by Nick Buckingham. Grouse, pheasant, duck, hare and above all venison all appear in due season. Recently Barbara had delicious roast partridge, cut off the bone and served with a wild mushroom sauce — succulent and tender, not tough and dry, as partridge can be. Nick serves venison with blood oranges or mushroom sauce, breast of chicken in a Roquefort cheese sauce, and fillet of beef with whisky and walnut sauce (very nice). His cooking is a blend of the artistic presentation and light touches of 'modern' French cooking and the generous portions and range of vegetables of traditional English.

He has oysters sent down by special delivery from the Isle of Mull. Another pleasant starter is his own smoked mackerel mousse with cucumber jelly. His soups are unusual and tasty — cream of fennel and orange, wild mushroom soup with lumpfish roe.

He produces some old dishes appreciated particularly up here in the Peaks, such as pig's head and trotters, salt beef and spice, made into brawn and served with red cabbage. But his sweets are especially popular, including a chocolate mousse, steamed coffee sponge with caramel sauce, cold Grand Marnier soufflé, lemon mousse with strawberry sauce in a brandy-snap basket and chocolate and fudge ice-cream with rum sauce.

English cheeses are served

with home-made walnut bread.

There are some gorgeous wines on the list, way beyond my means – a Château Latour 1967, two St Julien clarets (Beychevelle 1966 and Talbot 1970) and four rare, magnificent old Burgundies, bottled by Pierre Ponnelle in Beaune. The rarest is a Clos St Denis 1959 from the little village of Morey-St-Denis, whose wines are under-rated.

Barbara, addicted to white Burgundy, chose a heavyish Montagny 1982 from Louis Latour. The housewines, much cheaper, white and red, are Burgundies from Saint Aubin and the famous negociant Marc Raoul Clerget, so worth a trial. There is a house red from Bordeaux, too. Cheaper wines are few but well chosen.

An expensive but delightful Pouilly Fumé is on the list –

called Baron L, it is produced at Château du Nozet by Baron Patrick Ladoucette. Nice with oysters or pheasant. With venison or any of the stronger game I should choose in the medium range the Château La Cardonne 1979 (owned by Lafite-Rothschilds) or Clerget's 1982 Santenay, a Côte de Beaune.

In the park of one of the Stateliest Homes of England.

Chatsworth House, the Duke and Duchess of Devonshire's home, has one of the world's finest collections of paintings, furniture, tapestries, china, sculpture and gold and silver plate – almost overwhelming in its beauty and interest. It was collected by fifteen generations of Cavendishes, and although death duties forced the sale of a few items, it is virtually intact. The family lives in part of the house, which is administered by a Trust to ensure that it is preserved for the nation. It is open to the public from March 31–October 27 and a quick tour would take you an hour. The present house was built in 1687. Additions were made 1800–30. The 105-acre garden is famous for its landscape, lake, fountains and cascade. You may picnic or take your dog on a lead. The river Derwent runs through the grounds. The roof of the house covers 1.3 acres; there are 175 rooms, 17 staircases and 3,426 feet of passages. The Duchess has written a good guide, with fine colour pictures. It costs £1. At the farm shop one and a half miles away at Pilsley you can buy game from the estate and home-made pâté in season.

The village of Edensor (pronounced Ensor) is part of the estate. Mentioned in the Domesday Book of 1086, it was much destroyed and rebuilt in the nineteenth century by a Duke who did not want to see it from his park. The old farmhouse (now village store and post office) was left, the fourteenth century church destroyed. The present church was designed by Gilbert Scott in 1866. Buried in the churchyard is Kathleen Kennedy, sister of the late President Kennedy. She married the present Duke's elder brother William, who was killed in 1944 fighting in Normandy as a Guards' Officer. She was killed in an air crash in 1948. Also buried here is Joseph Paxton, gardener at Chatsworth, who designed the old Crystal Palace in glass, based on the great conservatory he had designed for Chatsworth.

This is the Peak District National Park, the first to be designated in 1951. The Park Authority is at Bakewell, five miles from the Cavendish. In a lovely setting of richly wooded hills, Bakewell has a superb arched and buttressed bridge built 700 years ago. You can still buy the famous Bakewell tarts in The Square. The wonderful Derbyshire Dales are within easy reach – Dovedale, Monk's Dale, Lathkill and Monsal Dale. It is some of the loveliest river valley country in England with peaks of rugged grandeur. Most beautiful is Dovedale, about twenty miles SW of Bakewell; here the river Dove flows fast through a wooded gorge. Three miles past Bakewell is Haddon Hall, a beautifully restored mediaeval manor.

Matlock (9m S of Chatsworth), spa resort on the Derwent among woodlands and hills, has dramatic views of peaks and crags. The Heights of Abraham above the town were named, by an officer who fought at Quebec under General Wolfe, after the Heights scaled there by the English in the battle.

Buxton (18m W of Chatsworth) is a spa 1,007 feet up but sheltered by higher peaks. Its magnificent Crescent was built in 1780 by the fifth Duke of Devonshire to rival the Crescent at Bath. The spring water, rich in nitrogen and carbon, flows at a temperature of 28°C (82°F) and unlike most spa water, is pleasant to drink.

**Chewton Glen
New Milton, Hampshire
BH25 6QS (off A35 from
Lyndhurst before
Christchurch and
Bournemouth).
Telephone: Highcliffe (04252)
5341.
DBB F (also suites);
SBB C, D, E.
Cheaper winter breaks.
Dinner D, E;
lunch B.
Open all year.
No children under 7.
No dogs.
Credit cards: Euro, Visa,
Amex, Diners.**

Chewton Glen is expensive –
and worth it. It is one of the best
hotels in the world, it has
improved every year since I
first stayed in 1968 and just has
to be in my list of favourites.

Martin Skan, who still calls
himself an 'amateur hotelier',
has achieved the near-
impossible since 1966 –
created an hotel with the
luxury, matchless service,
polish and refinement of Claridge's and yet as cosy, warm
and personal as an intimate
English country house hotel.
Like Claridge's, it is one of ten
British country house hotels in
the international Leading
Hotels of the World list of 195
hotels.

In thirty acres of impeccably-
kept gardens and lawns on the
edge of the New Forest, a mile
from the sea, it was converted
from a truly handsome old
house where last century Captain Frederick Marryat planned his novel 'Children of the
New Forest'. A mass of little
public rooms give it an
intimate feeling. Carpets, fabrics and furniture are luxurious
and every bedroom is individ-

ually planned and quite different from the next. We have
slept in several and each has
been a different experience.
My last had a bathroom up in a
gallery. Another has a round
bath in the middle of the bathroom. The suites made recently
from the coach house have
their own little patio gardens.

Iced water, fruit and sherry
await in the bedrooms, bathrobes in the bathroom. In the
dining room you eat from
Wedgwood china with silver-
plated cutlery and drink from
Dartington glass.

There are tennis courts, croquet, charming walks round
the grounds and a delightful
heated pool beneath a balustraded terrace. And a helipad.
But above all, the staff are
friendly and helpful when
needed, but know how to fade.
It is a superb hotel by any
country's standards.

*A Leading Hotel of
the World.*

Food & Drink

Chewton Glen has two rosettes for cooking from the AA, one from Egon Ronay, and one from Michelin. The restyled restaurant has fine oil paintings, table settings are a joy, the service perfect and the cooking of young Pierre Chevillard well worthy of his native France. All tastes are catered for, from light, airy and modern such as a delicate vegetable terrine, to some fine old-fashioned dishes, such as the superb Filet de Boeuf London House of Scottish fillet steak stuffed with foie gras, baked in pastry and served with a beautiful Périgourdine sauce. Salad

Forestière starter is an absolute joy to me – grilled breast of quail marinaded in red wine, served on a green salad with walnut-oil vinaigrette, cèpe mushrooms and potato. Pierre makes super ravioli stuffed with vegetable fennel, mushrooms and onion, too.

His straightforward cooking is excellent, too – best-end of English lamb roast with rosemary, grilled Dover sole, braised salmon with butter sauce. He serves a nice variety of potato dishes, too – genuine rösti, Gruyère potatoes and fondante. Everything is freshly cooked, of course, and guests who do not like lightly-cooked vegetables are invited to ask for

them cooked longer. He might even cook you English school boiled cabbage if you asked!

Breakfast croissants are excellent.

The wine cellar is one of the best in Britain, with more than 250 listed wines, cleverly chosen, some cheaper than in a lot of inferior hotels. You could pay £150 for a 1952 Château Lafite Rothschild, but I don't expect you will. There are a lot of highly drinkable wines around £10 (1985), such as Lamothe Cissac Haut Médoc. And from Côtes de Bourg, the unfashionable Bordeaux region where the wines nevertheless have body and a fruity flavour and can be drunk young, 1981

Château Guionne (one of the best) is cheap, so is the house St Emilion.

Do have a look at the splendid choice of Beaujolais. There are two scarce wines from smaller areas which are well worth trying – St Amour, a delightful wine from the Loron family's Domaine des Billards, best of the producers, and a Chénas of Château de Jean Loron. Chénas production is even smaller. With roasts or steak try the strong, beefy Morgon of Château de Raousset. For lighter dishes try the nice fruity Fleurie or the pleasant Juliénas '83 which I would have kept a bit longer to fill out.

Among a good and varied list of German wines are two genuine Trockenbeerenauslese, wine made from grapes not only with the 'noble rot' with superb fruit and acidity but allowed to dry on the vine until like raisins. The risk of leaving the grapes is enormous, the cost seven or eight times that of producing a fair quality Riesling, which is why it will cost you £60 to taste Graf Von Plettenberg's renowned Winzenheimer Rosenheck. I have never tasted it, alas.

For a middle priced red wine you cannot do much better with all the Chewton Glen choice than the 1976 Château La Lagune. All La Lagune wines of the 1970s were good value, and the 1976 was one of the fruitiest clarets I have tasted. A pity that I have drunk all mine!

Local Drives The New Forest (2m), Royal hunting forest of William the Conqueror, has 92,000 acres of trees, bushes, moorlands, streams and glades, with wild deer and ponies, and several stables where you can hire horses.

Beaulieu Abbey and Palace House (15m E), originally a Cistercian Abbey founded 1204 by King John, is now the home of Lord Montagu (in the old gatehouse). In the grounds is the National Motor Museum which he has built into the finest car museum in the world. It includes many historic racing cars, vintage and veteran cars, cycles and motorbikes. 3m S is Bucklers' Hard, village on Beaulieu estuary where ships were built for Nelson from New Forest oaks. It now has a maritime museum. Over the estuary at Exbury are 200 acre gardens, famous for azaleas and rhododendrons.

On the return drive to New Milton is Lymington on the Solent, with fine Georgian houses and yacht harbour. From here you can take a car across to the Isle of Wight (book ahead) for Cowes, the Royal yachting centre, and Osborne House, Queen Victoria's fascinating holiday home. Just north of Lymington at Boldre is the Red Lion Inn, with antiques, tapestries, prints and a display of chamber pots.

For night life, theatre, music and sport go to Bournemouth (10m W of Chewton), a genuine all-year seaside resort. At Poole (5m on, with a huge harbour) you can see pottery being made.

At Romsey (20m NE through New Forest) is Broadlands, home of the late Lord Louis Mountbatten, sailor, statesman, war hero and Allied Commander, whose grandson Lord Romsey lives there. A lovely Palladian house with riverside gardens by Capability Brown (open to the public). See also Lainston House, page 77.

There are twenty golf courses within twelve miles of Chewton Glen.

Clifton Hotel

Clifton Hotel
Viewfield Street, Nairn,
Nairnshire IV12 4HW
(from A96 Aberdeen–
Inverness road turn at the
roundabout in town onto the
Marine road above the beach.
Left at the end and the hotel is
on the first corner).
Telephone: Nairn (0667)
53119.
DBB −C;
BB −A (4 of 16 rooms have
bathroom but not wc).
Dinner: card only; B, C.
Closed December 1–March 1.
Credit cards: Euro, Visa,
Amex, Diners.

I never dreamed that I should fall for a Victorian house, with heavy Victorian furniture, knick-knacks, bric-à-brac, objets d'art, with rich hand-blocked wallpapers half smothered with pictures and paintings, and chandeliers. But I had not stayed in one so stylishly and sympathetically furnished and decorated by a near-eccentric aesthete like Gordon MacIntyre and an understanding artist like his wife Muriel, a well-known potter. Nor had I found an hotel which is a licensed theatre, with performances by famous musicians, and professional actors. The Provost who built it in 1877 might well be shocked.

It all fits perfectly into this seaside resort on the Moray Firth where you expect to see Victorian children in sailor suits with nannies crossing the green sward to the long curving sandy beach, and where on the Marine road is a pure Victorian bandstand beside the cricket pitch with a tiny pavilion marked 'Nairn County Cricket Club'. Did W. G. Grace play here?

A newish dining room, with split levels and views over the garden to the sea and hills of Ross beyond, becomes the theatre in winter months. The little green lunch room is very pretty. The big bar lounge is comfortably handsome. The huge main lounge, with ornate hand-blocked wallpaper that was used in the Robing Room in the Palace of Westminster in 1849, is a marvellous Victorian fantasia. I wish John Betjeman had seen it.

Bedrooms, all individually designed, vary from suites and big rooms with huge four-posters to my little room with bright flowery paper, shower, basin and a mysterious glass-covered pillar cunningly hiding the loo.

The atmosphere is of a well-run private house with foibles. If you refuse to be captivated, you will at least be interested.

Delightful and different
– art and old lace.

Food & Drink

The menu is in French, the ingredients are decidedly Scottish, the cooking of Forbes Stutt has well earned the AA's rosette. Dinner is *à la carte* but inexpensive. Tables are spread with delicate lace covers, you drink from crystal, eat off bone china and the service is attentive without being irritating.

Eight starters include almost-local oysters in season and an outstanding smoked salmon, smoked by a friend of Gordon's. Other outstanding dishes are prawns and mushrooms in real cream, salmon trout in jelly, Stilton mousse.

My soup of leeks and carrots, puréed in clotted cream, was absolutely delicious. I followed with wild salmon from a local river. It was succulent, chewy with a delicious flavour. There are plenty of good salmon rivers around here, including the Spey itself. These Scottish chefs are a bit spoiled for ingredients, with so much fresh white fish, shellfish (including lobster), salmon, wild and farmed trout, river crayfish, free-range chickens and ducks, Angus beef, field-reared veal, Scottish lamb, loads of game, on which the Clifton prides itself particularly, and superb fresh vegetables. I cannot see Nouvelle Cuisine taking on in Scotland. Most Scots would lynch the chef!

There is excellent soft fruit, too, especially strawberries and raspberries. I had a delightful concoction of the lightest possible sponge with fresh raspberries, cream and Drambuie.

Dinner at the Clifton is remarkable value.

The list of over 200 wines is excellently chosen. It is strong in middle-range Bordeaux, and shows knowledgeable variety especially among lesser known wines of France.

With salmon I had a delicate Rully, with a sort of nutty flavour, from Jean-François Délorme's Domaine de la

Renarde. He has put Rully wines back on to good lists. There was also one of his reds, 1977, on the list at a low price and a light fruity red Givry which I much prefer to most wines of its neighbour Mercurey, and which would go well with anything from lobster or salmon to duck or lamb.

There are also well chosen bargain-priced Italians, and some wines from Central and Southern France seen little in Britain, including a much under-rated Bandol Mas de la Rouvière 1976 produced by the Bunan family, also a rarish, prized, still Champagne (Coteaux Champenoise) – Ruinart Chardonnay. Among Rhône wines is a 1977 Cornas, a dark wine which matures well in bottle after a rough start, and a white Condrieu, an interesting wine made from a rare Viognier grape grown on a soil of powdered rock which often gets washed down the slopes and has to be replaced!

This is a good hotel for anyone interested in wine without a fortune to spend.

LOCAL DRIVES

Nairn is on the Moray Firth, North-east of Inverness (16m). It has an old fishertown with walks along the Nairn river. Eastward, back from the sandy foreshore, is undisturbed Culbin Forest, planted in sand dunes once called the Scottish Sahara. The best approach is from Kintersack, signposted from A96 just before Forres. Fine wildlife, including roe deer, badgers, and capercaillie, Britain's largest game bird, which is like a small turkey. Kincorth House nearby has gardens with gorgeous roses.

Several castles round here, including Cawdor (5m SW of Nairn), drawbridge, portcullis and dungeons, built in the fourteenth century by the family who still live there; scene of Duncan's murder in Macbeth; Brodie Castle (8m E by A96, National Trust for Scotland, eighteenth–nineteenth century furniture); Balvenie Castle, Dufftown (39m from Nairn by A96 to Elgin, then A941), one of Scotland's largest and best preserved; fourteenth century, it was owned in succession by Comyns family, then Douglases, finally the Atholls; Edward I stayed in 1304, Mary Queen of Scots in 1562; a mile away are Balvenie and Glenfiddich whisky distilleries); Castle Grant (near Grantown – enlarged in the eighteenth century by the Adam brothers) – not open to public.

Culloden (14m W of Nairn off A96) is the sad moorland where in 1746 Charles Edward Stuart, seeking George II's throne, thrust 5,000 wet, march-weary Highlanders into hopeless battle against experienced troops of the Duke of Cumberland. 1,200 Highlanders were slaughtered. You can see stones of mass graves. The Information Centre has films and charts of the battle.

I am very fond of Inverness (16m), an attractive town on the river Ness and the Caledonian canal, which joins the Moray Firth with Loch Ness. A superb theatre, Eden Court, made from a Bishop's palace, has lawns to the river. The canal is a pleasure craft centre. Drive round Loch Ness to Fort Augustus and back on the other bank. The Monster research centre is on the north bank near Drumnadrochit.

Combe House Hotel

Combe House
Gittisham, near Honiton,
Devon
EX14 0AD
(3½m from Honiton; take A30
towards Exeter then lane
(signposted) where road is
double tracked).
Telephone: Honiton (0404)
2756.
DBB C–D;
suite E;
SBB A.
Dinner C–D.
Open all year.
Dogs allowed but not in dining
room.
Credit cards: Euro, Visa,
Amex, Diners.

True seclusion and tranquillity in this Elizabethan mansion in 3,500 acres of park and woodland. Stand on the terrace looking down to the long drive which takes you to the nearest lane, with hardly another building in sight, and you feel as if you are 100 miles from noise and modern living. Yet it is only one and a half miles along narrow lanes from the busy A30 and thirteen miles from Exeter.

It is a superb and stately home, replacing a fourteenth-century house, among eight and a half acres of gardens with old and beautiful trees, including cedars, lovely azaleas and rhododendrons.

It has been restored by John Boswell, direct descendant of James Boswell, chronicler of Dr Johnson's idiosyncrasies, and he brought with him much of the furniture and paintings from the Boswell ancestral home in Scotland. More antique furniture, panelling, doors, paintings and coats of arms have survived from previous owners. And Thérèse Boswell, John's wife, has added murals. Her artist's sense of colour has made both the smallish dining rooms and the bedrooms into bright but peaceful and relaxing rooms. The bar is decorated with pictures of John's racehorses.

The entrance lounge, the original Great Hall of the mansion, is most impressive, with Delft tiles round the fireplace and superb panelling and pictures. There are many fine fireplaces in this house.

The views from some windows sweep over the Blackdown Hills as far as Exmoor but you have no need to leave the estate for peaceful walks amid pastures, woods rich in game, and along the little river Otter, jumping with brown trout. You can fish over one and a half miles of the south bank but only with dry fly. You can ride horses, too, from the estate farm. It is just the place to live the life of country gentlefolk, if only temporarily.

A true country gentleman's estate

Food & Drink

The dining rooms are elegant, Thérèse Boswell's cooking is genuine Cordon Bleu, service is cheerful and fairly informal and the atmosphere that of dinner at a house party weekend.

Menus are changed regularly and supplemented with two to four dishes of the day. Last time we were there a starter was an excellent avocado and prawn thermidor. Fish is very good, particularly prawn thermidor and Dover sole served several ways – mornay, meunière, with smoked salmon butter and a delightful dish called Dover Sole Mère Recamier (breadcrumbed and deep fried, with the bone removed and filled with seafood and cream sauce).

Chicken breasts flamed in Pernod, are served in a creamy sauce of shrimp, scampi, prawn, white wine and vermouth.

Mrs Boswell deserves her coveted AA rosette for cooking. Many Devonians drive some miles to dine here.

The wine list is short, and very interesting. Most wines are good value. John Boswell is proud of his red and white housewines, which are cheap and are obtainable in half or whole bottles and magnums.

The red has excellent flavour. The white is a little heavy and sweetish as an aperitif, but would go well with the sole.

It is difficult to know which claret to choose to accompany, let us say, the chicken, the sirloin grilled over an open fire, or the lamb cutlets. There is a very fruity Graves with a strong bouquet, St Gerome 1978; a 1978 St Emilion Grand Cru of which I have sunk many a barrel, Les Grandes Murailles; a Château Beychevelle 1977 from the St Julien vineyard which produces, blessedly, a lot of wine – 1977 was not considered to be one of Beychevelle's greatest vintages but

it has developed with time; an unusual Margaux called Domaine de Fontarnay 1979, which is the second wine of Château Brane-Cantenac, made from younger vines and, I am told, has a lot of its elder brother's flavour.

All these are cheap or middle-priced wines. The great wines, like 1967 Cheval Blanc St Emilion, are much cheaper than the current market price.

There is a very good really dry Graves white from the home of my ancestors, Leognan. It is called Château Carbonnieux and could well be drunk as an aperitif, with fishy starters, like the fish hors d'oeuvres, local scallops or sole. The 1982 white Rully Burgundy is good value. Among dearer red Burgundies is a gorgeous 1977 Chambertin, for me the greatest of Burgundies; this one is from Tapet, one of the best of the two dozen owners. Then there is a fruity, cheapish Fleurie regarded there as the best – Domaine des Quatre Vents, splendid with salmon, chicken, scallops or prawn thermidor.

Only forty-two table wines from which to choose, but there is no shortage of good choice!

On the hotel reception desk is a file of places of interest in the area. Honiton (3½m) is now bypassed by big roads and is tranquil again, with fine Georgian buildings in its main street. You can see lace in one shop. Honiton was famous for it from sixteenth to nineteenth centuries and a little lace-making survives. An important livestock market is held on Tuesdays, a street market on Tuesdays and Saturdays.

The coast is seven miles S from Gittisham at Sidmouth (Regency and early Victorian resort) and Beer (fishing village in a little bay). Beer Head, 426ft high, has the westernmost chalk cliffs on the Channel coast. Branscombe (2½m W of Beer) is a village of character and beauty. Mediaeval farmhouses, cottages of cob and thatch, an old forge and bakery are sited on slopes of a steep wooded valley which widens towards the sea. The attractive church has Norman

tower and nave, thirteenth-century transepts and a three-tier Georgian pulpit.

Axminster (10m from Honiton on A35) has made carpets since 1755 – started by a man who had learned from the Turks. A market town, Musbury (2½m SW) was the seat of the Drake family (cousins of Francis Drake) from fifteenth to eighteenth centuries and in the church painted effigies of three generations kneel in prayer. They lived at an earlier version of Ashe House nearby, and Elizabeth Drake married a certain Winston Churchill. Their son John Churchill was born here. He became the Duke of Marlborough, probably Britain's greatest-ever soldier, and ancestor of Sir Winston Churchill. With Drake blood, no wonder Sir Winston was such a fire-eater.

Lyme Regis (5½m past Axminster) has been a delightful resort since the eighteenth century. Jane Austen used to stay and write here. Originally a mediaeval port which got its royal title 'Regis' because Edward I used its protected harbour when fighting the French. The Duke of Monmouth landed here in 1685 to lead his ill-fated rebellion against James II. Then Lyme took to smuggling.

For Exeter (13m), Bicton Park, Killerton Gardens, see Woodhayes Hotel, Whimple, page 160. For Dartmoor, see Prestbury House Hotel, Bovey Tracey, page 127.

Congham Hall
Grimston,
King's Lynn,
Norfolk
PE32 1AH
(*not* at Congham; A148 from
King's Lynn; right on small
road signposted Grimston).
Telephone: Hillington (0485)
600250.
DBB C–D;
suite E;
SBB B–C;
suite C.
Dinner 8 courses D–E;
lunch A.
Cheaper weekend breaks.
Closed 2 weeks after
Christmas.
Dogs in kennels.
Stabling and hay for horses.
No young children.
Credit cards: Euro, Visa,
Amex, Diners.

Congham Hall is one of the most handsome hotels I have seen. But I am addicted to lovely white Georgian houses with pretty flower gardens, a park, orchards, a herb garden, and especially with horses in the stables. Congham has all these in forty-four acres, plus its own cricket pitch with a thatched pavilion, a small swimming pool and a tennis court. It is only seven miles from the charming market town of King's Lynn.

What a gorgeous home it would make! And is *was* the home of Lady Meriel Howarth until Trevor and Christine Forecast made it into an hotel.

The alterations and redecorating they have done are thoughtful and sympathetic – quite in keeping with a Georgian house. I love the dining room in true Regency pink (not *prawn* pink, as an acidic Guide reported!). Bedrooms, all completely equipped and relaxing, include a suite with a lounge and balcony. There is a non-Georgian jacuzzi-spa bath, too.

Businessmen visiting King's Lynn usually take some rooms in the week. Weekends are especially tranquil and special cheap terms are offered for weekend breaks.

The service is skilled – efficient without being slick.

Food&Drink

The distinguished chef John McGeever may be an enthusiast for Nouvelle dishes as well as English, but he does not believe in half-starving you. Some suggest, even, that his eight-course dinners are for 'greedy people who like rich food'. They are talking about me again!

The first five courses are really a series of snack starters, in the manner of the new fashionable 'tasting' menus in France. And very tasty these are. Such delights as hot fried goat's cheese and fig, strips of raw fillet beef, smoked haddock and sweetbread tart, local shrimps with orange and mustard butter in pastry, smoked trout mousse in smoked halibut, lovely fresh terrines, hot chicken liver and wild mushrooms in Madeira sauce.

Soups are super – a choice of beef and mushroom consommé, perhaps, chicken and almond, or chilled carrot and orange cream. Between soup and main course, sorbet is served for the digestion's sake. I am a great believer in this – especially with a glass of Calvados. It works for me.

John believes implicitly in local fish and meat and makes his own vinegars, pickles and chutneys for his sauces. These are modern style, many invented by him. You might get lamb's liver with grapefruit and raspberry vinegar, pork with two pepper sauces, venison with pickled pears and a port sauce, duck with Pernod and ginger sauce with fresh figs. The main course decides the meal price. A good choice of cheeses and freshly-made sweets follow, then coffee.

Lunch with plenty of choice and more traditional English cooking, including a much-favoured steak and kidney pie, is splendid value. All is fresh; nothing frozen.

For breakfast, honey comes from the estate, bread is home-made, so are crab-apple jelly and jams from fruit grown on the estate. There are few hotels outside Britain, even in France, which can make a boast like this.

Trevor Forecast has a down-to-earth attitude to wine. He has two lists – a house selection, with low prices for an hotel of this standard, including some well-chosen wines between £5 and £10 a bottle and the majority £12. Then there is a connoisseurs' list, not much over £12, culminating in a 1971 Château Haut-Brion, £45 at my last viewing.

With Burgundy prices rising far too fast through US and Japanese buying, claret prices rising because of disasters in the 1984 vintage when St Emilion in particular was hit hard by the weather, and Chancellors milking the wine-bibber harder than ever, Trevor Forecast is doing what all but the most luxurious and expensive hotels will have to do soon – buying more Spanish Rioja, which has improved enormously in fifteen years, and wines of the South of France which will surprise people who do not know them with their quality and strength.

 The Royal Estate at Sandringham is five miles away. An ugly Victorian house bought by Edward VII who had unhappy memories of Osborne House in the Isle of Wight. Some rooms, the park and motor museum are open when the family are not there. The royal parish church is interesting for the rich gifts given by Royals and others. Not many village churches have a solid silver altar (gift of an American, Rodman Wanamaker), a pulpit covered in silver, jewelled Bible, and solid gold and jewelled communion plate. Wolferton, once the royal railway station, is now disused and a museum of Royal railway travel.

King's Lynn (7m), busy town, seaport, market centre (Saturday and Tuesday), has many old buildings, including huge eleventh-century St Margaret's church in white limestone, a chequered flint Guildhall (1421), and a Custom House (1683). The son of one custom's officer, George Vancouver, navigated the north coast of Western America in 1790. The city and island were called after him.

Norwich (38m from Grimston) was one of the largest cities in England when the Normans invaded. It is rich in old treasures, including a magnificent spired cathedral with a huge close

running down to the river Wensum, the Castle (now a museum), Strangers' Hall, a fourteenth-century mansion turned into a museum of domestic life, and a charming Victorian-style mustard shop (Colmans, of course).

Newmarket (45m): racecourse, training stables, Jockey Club HQ (1772), National Stud (open Sunday afternoons, mornings of race days).

Cambridge (52m from Grimston): a university town for 700 years, it is beautiful and enchanting. Buy a local guide book.

Coast NE is interesting. See Holkham Hall, W of Wells-next-the-Sea, magnificent eighteenth-century Palladian Mansion, seat of the 'modern' Earls of Leicester of Holkham, for whom the great architect Kent rebuilt it in 1734; son of the first Earl was Coke of Norfolk, great agricultural reformer. Paintings by Rubens, Van Dyck, Poussin, Gainsborough; seventeenth–eighteenth-century tapestry and furniture; Greek and Roman statuary; over 4,000 items of bygone days, such as ploughs, tools, fire engines, steam engines, kitchens, dairy, smithy (open May 30–September 30 afternoons Sunday, Monday, Thursday; Wednesday in July, August).

I wish I owned it – including the cricket pitch.

Elcot Park Hotel
Elcot, near Newbury,
Berkshire
RG16 8NJ (5m W of Newbury
on A4 Newbury–Bath road;
4m E of Hungerford; M4 exits
13 and 14 7m).
Telephone: Kintbury (0488)
58100.
DBB C–D;
SBB B.
Dinner B–C.
Open all year.
Credit cards: Euro, Visa,
Amex, Diners.

This grand and dignified house of 1678, with Georgian additions, stands in sixteen acres of well-kept grounds, with a fine terrace for summer drinking or lazing, great log fires burning in chillier weather. It is a peaceful hideout for exploring many interesting places, such as Oxford, Ascot, Winchester, Marlborough and Bath.

The lovely grounds were laid out in 1848 by William Paxton, gardener at Chatsworth, designer of the Crystal Palace, and Royal Gardener to Queen Victoria. He planted many rare trees and superb shrubs. In spring hundreds of thousands of daffodils bloom. There is a tennis court.

Bedrooms are especially attractive, individually furnished with old furniture and fine drapes, always elegant and some luxurious. All have good bathrooms. Our room had a draped double bed, a grand old wardrobe with plenty of space. A little annexe room with lovely views overlooking the Kennet valley had a settee, writing table and chairs. The walls were covered in slubbed silk. In the bathroom there was not only a hairdryer but a bath pillow. This hotel is a member of the French association Relais du Silence – promising quiet, peace and rest.

We are both surprised that it has not yet had much recognition. Small executive conferences are sometimes held there, but they do not obtrude and help Harold and June Sterne to keep up their high standards of service and meals out of season. I only hope that the executives in conference do not take exception to offers of hot air ballooning. There are several special 'getaway breaks', including one called Four Poster Romance, with champagne, flowers, a special dinner and breakfast in bed.

Food & Drink

In a Regency-style restaurant the Sternes serve meals much above the standard that we expected for the price and the hotel's lack of stars for cuisine. Neville Pease, the chef, offers fairly straightforward cooking with many personal touches. His hot salmon mousse, his poached pears wrapped in smoked salmon and served with his own special lemon mayonnaise, monkfish tails, very like fresh crayfish, with fresh lime sauce, guinea fowl stuffed with veal and spinach in Madeira sauce, and his rack of lamb with minted béarnaise sauce were all praised by guests and show his inventiveness. He serves a lovely freshwater crayfish soup laced with brandy and a smoked chicken and spinach mousse.

At our last dinner the set-price menu (very good value) had baked fresh salmon cream among five starters, then cream of leek soup, followed by a choice of six main courses which included the superb fresh Kennet trout and honey-roast duckling with orange and cherry sauce.

The English cheeses are a joy – six, all from unpasteurized milk mostly made on the farm. There is a blue Stilton from Colston Bassett, said to be the only unpasteurized Stilton, a year old farm cheddar from Somerset, a Somerset natural farm cheese with chives running through it (Wedmore), a Sleight Farm goat cheese, a Shropshire blue and a most interesting Somerset cheese called Tornegus, cured for three months in fragrant herbs and white wine from Penshurst in Kent – fruity, herby, mellow and unique.

Neville Pease offers to grill meat or fish for anyone who asks for it. It would need to be a good grill to make us miss his special dishes.

There are plenty of very

drinkable AC (Appellation Controlée) wines on the list at lowish prices, such as Chablis, Pouilly-Fumé among whites, Fleurie 1983, a St Emilion and a strong Châteauneuf-du-Pape 1978 among the reds.

Among medium-priced wines I would try the 1980 AC Nuits-St-Georges with any of the meat dishes or the honeyroast duckling. You do not see many ordinary Nuits about these

days – only dearer first growths, but this one is good and strong with a super smell.

There is a special selection of bin ends, mostly of fairly pricey fine clarets, such as a 1963 Château de Heby and a lovely Margaux, Château Prieuré-Lichine 1981. This

property was a bit run-down when Alexis Lichine moved there from Château Lascombes in 1952, but he has improved the wine enormously, although I would give this one a few more years yet. Some of the wines have taken twelve years to reach their best.

Superb house, lovely park, excellent value

Newbury has a first-grade racecourse, and Ascot is only thirty-six miles away. The Berkshire Downs around here are training grounds for some of our finest racehorses, and strings of them can be seen exercising. Most stables are at Lambourn, twelve miles NW. Newbury became famous when Jack of Newbury set up as a clothier, finally employing 1,000 people. You can see the remains of his house in Northbrook Street where he entertained Henry VII and later Catherine of Aragon, wife of Henry VIII. He and his son rebuilt St Nicholas Church (1532), in Perpendicular style, spacious and airy, with a lovely pulpit. Over the Kennet by a little old bridge is the lovely old Wool Hall with superb woodwork – now a museum of antiquities.

Many pretty villages round here include Boxford (4m NW

Newbury), thatched roofs, weathered tiles, stream; Brightwalton (10m NW), among lanes and hills in heart of Berkshire Downs; Blewbury (15m N), with old town of narrow lanes, old pubs, white cottages and a mansion, Hall Barn, which was a hunting lodge of Henry VIII; Bucklebury (5m NE), old village in river Pang valley with a mile long avenue of oaks and a common where 20,000 Parliamentarian troops camped before the second battle of Newbury in 1644 (Civil War).

Hungerford (4m W of Elcot) is on both the river Kennet and the Kennet and Avon Canal and has been known for trout and crayfish since the fourteenth century. The Bear Inn (established 1297) was owned by two of Henry VIII's wives – Anne of Cleves and Catherine Howard. Now known for its good wine cellar. Many antique shops.

Marlborough (15m W) is a handsome old town with Georgian buildings, alleys of earlier timbered cottages, and a broad High Street, partly arcaded. Alongside is the ancient Savernake Forest, old Royal hunting forest, still with deer, rare birds, superb old trees, including four mile long Grand Avenue, almost arcaded, and wild flowers.

Wantage (13m N) was the birthplace of Alfred the Great in 849AD. It has seventeenth–eighteenth-century buildings and narrow streets, one leading from Newbury Street has cobbles of sheep's bones. In the thirteenth-century church of Saints Peter and Paul are tombs of Fitzwaryn family into which Dick Whittington married.

For Oxford (31m) see Weston Manor Hotel, Weston-on-the-Green, page 154. For Bath (41m) see Homewood Park Hotel, Hinton Charterhouse, page 62.

THE FEATHERS HOTEL·

**The Feathers Hotel
Market Street,
Woodstock, Oxfordshire
OX7 1SX
(main shopping street off
A34).
Telephone: Woodstock (0993)
812291.
DBB C–F;
SBB B–C.
Dinner C;
lunch A.
Open all year.
Credit cards: Euro, Visa,
Amex, Diners.**

But for its dignity and sophistication, the Feathers, with its maze of secretive passageways and many staircases, would make a fine setting for a bed-to-bed farce. The new name comes from the stuffed birds which you meet in the bar, the reception and on the stairs. It has had a complicated history since the seventeenth century with tales of four separate houses, one a butcher's shop where the stone-floored reception now is and of local bigwigs being driven in their carriages through the tall archway to the door of their grand townhouse. It was also an inn called the Dorchester Arms. The little town of Woodstock has always been rich in inns, as befits the seat of the Churchill family, and currently has sixteen to serve 2,000 inhabitants – and visitors to Blenheim Palace.

Gordon Campbell-Gray, who came from a château-hotel in Holland in 1983, has made the Feathers the most elegant of the sixteen despite the deserved popularity of the Bear. As a mark of neighbourliness, no doubt, Jane Spencer-Churchill

helped with the interior decorating and the result is stunning. Apart from the superb blending of colours, the fine antique furniture and pictures, prints, china and antiquarian books positioned most thoughtfully, fireplaces have been opened up, hand-hewn beams and old stonework revealed, old pine panelling restored to make the whole house appear that it has stayed unchanged through the centuries.

The green bar is charming, even with a stuffed buzzard as company. In summer you can drink in the courtyard. Bedrooms are all different, many with antique furniture. Ours had interesting pictures, one by Isaac Cook. The bathroom had very hot water and good large towels – big enough for me. Dividing pillars give the dining room more intimacy and the chairs are high-backed and comfortable. In a very short time, the Feathers has become recognised as a great little hotel and well deserves its AA rating of two red stars and a rosette for cooking.

Food & Drink

Both lunch and dinner menus are really excellent value. Eating from the card is not much dearer and there are some delicious starters.

Recently from the dinner menu Barbara chose a salad of smoked chicken, avocado and pink grapefruit in a honey dressing. Instead of salmon supreme or sirloin steak she chose venison because the Feathers is already renowned for cooking game. The meat was in small slices in a port wine sauce with glazed apple and a side plate of four fresh vegetables – courgettes, new potatoes, red cabbage and duchesse potatoes creamed with garlic and creamed spinach in the centre. Instead of a sweet she chose a savoury – prunes stuffed with water chestnuts, grilled wrapped in bacon. She said that it was superb.

But I am not a prune man and the sweets are good. If you can face the name, try tangerine dream – tangerine, cream, Cointreau and cream cheese between slices of shortbread in tangerine sauce.

Among the card starters are hot leek soufflé, cream of pea and pear soup, game pie of venison and pheasant with pistachio nuts in Cumberland sauce, Brie cheese marinaded in wine and herbs and deep fried in puff pastry, and the Feathers salad – smoked goose breast, red cabbage, carrot, orange, celery, cucumber, pine kernels and crispy bacon in honey dressing. Nouvelle chefs would make a meal of that.

The wine list is interesting, especially the clarets. Interesting cheap wines, too, like the Côtes-du-Rhône from the Caves de Vignerons, Vacqueras 1983. I thought that my family and I had drunk all that when we stayed in a farmhouse in a vineyard two miles up the road from the Caves in October 1984!

The dry white house wine, a Touraine Sauvignon, makes a nice aperitif and would go well with most starters. If you believe that one good smoke deserves another, there is an outstanding Pouilly-Fumé to drink with the smoked chicken or goose – Les Roches.

Among clarets is an excellently-priced good Margaux, a 1979 La Tour-de-Mons, and a 1977 Talbot for very little more. Both superb with the steak or venison. Plenty of really good dearer older clarets, too, like a delightful 1973 Château Palmer rated officially a third growth Margaux but for my money – and that of a lot of very great experts – rivalling often the great first growths.

Among Burgundies there is one of the best first growth Beaunes, Les Bressandes 1970 and the best Givry, a delicate fruity wine from Domaine du Baron Thenard, for drinking with such dishes as escalope of veal and breast of pheasant or of chicken.

The list of bin ends usually includes some mature wines at medium prices. Altogether, a good place to eat and drink. Take someone who really enjoys red wine.

A gem – in a fine setting.

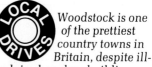

LOCAL DRIVES

Woodstock is one of the prettiest country towns in Britain, despite ill-advised modern building; Blenheim Palace, home of the Dukes of Marlborough and birthplace of Winston Churchill, is a treasure house which you can spend many hours exploring; and Oxford is only eight miles away. So there is little need to use much petrol.

The old houses of Woodstock, dating from the twelfth century, are largely of Cotswold stone. Market Street, in which the Feathers stands, has many shops selling antiques, china, silverware and handicrafts and is fascinating to window-shoppers.

Blenheim Palace is open from mid-March to October 31. You can have a guided tour or wander independently, but you will take the minimum of an hour and will probably want a week. A grandiose masterpiece designed by Sir John Vanbrugh, the artist, playwright and soldier, it is in gardens and park-like grounds by Capability Brown and is as original and well preserved as Versailles. From the grand hall to the saloon and all the state rooms it is so sumptuous and so full of treasures of historic and aesthetic interest that the first visit is overwhelming and you have to return. The tapestries are a particular joy to me. The room in which Winston Churchill was born on November 30, 1874 seems fairly simple. 'At Blenheim I took two very

important decisions,' he said, 'to be born and to be married. I am happily content with the decisions I took on both occasions.'

Queen Anne was to give Blenheim, on behalf of a grateful nation, to our greatest soldier, the Duke of Marlborough for four great victories over the French, especially over French and Bavarians at Blenheim in 1704. Vanbrugh designed and began the building, but fell out with the formidable Duchess and his assistant Hawksmoor finished it. Meanwhile Anne, who had also fallen out with the Duchess, would not pay the last £5,000 (about £5 million now) and the Duke had to pay himself. National gratitude did not survive long after the victory, as his descendant Winston Churchill was to find in 1945. Looking at the vast building, you can recall Vanbrugh's epitaph – 'Lie heavy on him, Earth, for he laid many heavy loads on thee'.

The park is open all the year. The new butterfly and plant centre is joined to the palace by a narrow-gauge railway. On the great lake a motor launch gives rides in season. Overlooking the lake is an arboretum with unusual trees.

At Bladon, two miles S of Woodstock, in St Martin's churchyard, Winston Churchill and his wife are buried, next to his father Lord Randolph Churchill and his mother, Jenny Jerome, the beautiful daughter of an American newspaper owner. Nearby are buried his son Randolph and daughters Sarah and Diana.

For Oxford, see Weston Manor, Weston-on-the-Green, page 154.

Granville Hotel

Granville Hotel
St Margarets Bay, near Dover,
Kent CT15 6OX
(5m N of Dover on A258 then
B2058).
Telephone: Dover (0304)
852212.
DBB A;
SBB A;
2 family rooms (3–4 beds).
A few rooms without private
bathrooms.
Dinner and lunch A.
Open all year.
Credit cards: Euro, Visa,
Amex, Diners.

The Granville Hotel applied for
AA recognition in late 1985.

A superlative position on the cliffs five miles from Dover's ferries to France and Belgium, with superb Channel views, a Relais du Silence offering peace and quiet, and remarkably good value – these are my reasons for choosing Eric Warner's fairly modest but convenient and friendly hotel.

It is not as luxurious as most of the hotels I have chosen but it is comfortable, clean and warm. You will get no grande cuisine, but some of the best value for money we have found in Britain.

The Victorian house has white balustraded balconies and partly-enclosed terrace looking out to sea. Four acres of lawns, paths, flowers and trees lead to a cliff edge with steps to a little sheltered beach. Or you can drive to the beach. Noël Coward had a house down there in pre-war days when St Margarets Bay and nearby Sandwich were the hideouts of stage and screen stars and millionaires. The army was at the Granville in the Second World War, defending Britain against invasion, including Private Peter Ustinov (see *Dear Me*, his autobiography). Now the garden has a lily pond with a little bridge – true peace.

Channel swimmers use the bay as the shortest distance to France (just under twenty miles). On clear days you can genuinely read the time on the town hall clock in Calais through U-boat binoculars on the bar terrace. A large compass from a Spanish galleon aids orientation. Golfers use the pleasant bar, decorated with pictures of old liners that used to pass this way, like the *Empress of Britain*, as a nineteenth hole after playing local courses at Kingsdown, Deal and two Sandwich courses, Princes and Royal St George's, scene of Sandy Lyle's Open Championship triumph.

The lounge and TV lounge are pleasantly furnished with antiques and pictures. There are few ornaments in the bedrooms, which makes them a little stark, though bright, with clean white furniture, and pretty tub chairs. Ours recently had windows on two sides overlooking the sea and gardens.

Food & Drink

The young French chef Christian Ory from Nantes cooks straightforward dishes deliciously for an unbelievably cheap set-price dinner with four choices on each course, and for his slightly more ambitious card. The meals are served in a very pleasant dining room with mahogany tables, Regency striped chairs, golden wallpaper with hunting prints and a view of the sea. In summer, lunch is sometimes served on the terrace looking down to the bay.

With so much stress on inventive dishes these days, it is easy to forget just how perfectly traditional dishes can be cooked. Local duckling and chicken are fresh each day at the Granville, and Christian's honey roast duckling in orange sauce was near perfection on our last visit. So was sole meunière with Dover sole, of course, which also come fresh each day from Deal, a fine town for fish, Dover itself, or Folkestone. Some superb shellfish comes fresh from Rye.

He is a very good soup chef, whether it is a white onion soup or his soupe de poissons served with garlic bread. Another starter, crêpe de jambon, with ham in a cream sauce, is in a different world from some you get.

He also serves duckling with a gooseberry sauce sometimes. The sweet and sour charcutière sauce served with pork chop is delightful. Sweets from the trolley include a really light crème caramel, but if there are two of you, try the delicious crêpes Suzette, made by the French waitress, Laurence.

I should like to taste some of Christian's more complicated dishes, even if they cost more.

The wine list was in a little disarray at our last visit for good reason. Eric Warner was just restocking because most of his better and older wines had been drunk dry. I am not surprised considering their prices – under £20 for Lafite-Rothschild, a delicious Meursault for just over £10 and an 1982 Fourchaumes Chablis – a really good one from Lamblin at Château de Milly – for under £10.

That was in the autumn of 1985. He also had a very drinkable red Macon as housewine at £3.95 and a better Côtes du Rhône Les Grangères for £4.20. All his wines, from Mouton Cadet (the popular blend from Rothschild) to the Moët et

Chandon Champagne, are 25–50 per cent below the average good hotel and restaurant prices. If he can replenish with a few good wines at reasonable prices and keep up the standards of value for meals cooked by Christian, I can see a lot of traditionalist eaters and drinkers making their way to the Channel shore for breaks off-season – especially with the chance of a cheap day-trip to France for some duty-free.

Incidentally, you can try one of the very best English white wines at the Granville – produced in small quantities and mostly sold direct from the vineyards near Canterbury – Staple St James Huxelrebe medium, rich and fruity.

A peaceful pad to eat and sleep en route to France.

LOCAL DRIVES

A wealth of places and things to see.

Sandwich (12m): an original Cinque Port given privileges in return for providing ships to defend England. Now two miles from sea (huge beach) because river Stour silted up. Lovely mediaeval buildings; town gate from 1384; timbered town hall 1579. Deal (6m), another Cinque port with Georgian houses and clover leaf castle built by Henry VIII. Goodwin Sands (which can swallow ships which go aground) five miles offshore. Between the pier and the famous lifeboat station (visits) is the spot where Julius Caesar landed in 55BC. Similar castle at Walmer, one mile S, is official residence of the warden of the Cinque Ports – an honour held at times by the Duke of Wellington, William Pitt, Winston Churchill, and Elizabeth, the Queen Mother (open daily). Inland off A2 Dover–Canterbury road is Barfreston with a village church built in 1080, carved inside and out with weird faces, animals playing musical instruments, birds and leaves.

Dover (5m): twelfth-century Norman castle built on Roman foundations; still contains stone Roman pharos (lighthouse) – open daily.

Canterbury (20m NW): Romans built a town here on the river Stour. In 603AD Augustine, consecrated a cathedral on the site of an old British church where he had baptised King Ethelbert of Kent. In 1007 Lanfranc, friend of William the Conqueror, started the long grey building, Mother Church of all Anglicans. It has survived fires, wars, desecration by Puritans and bombing by Germans. Beautiful thirteenth-century glass windows show scenes from miracles. Modern windows are by Hungarian artist Ernest Bossanyi. See also the tomb of Edward, the Black Prince, who defeated the French at Crécy, the lovely twelfth-century choir with fourteenth-century screen, and the Norman crypt. Trinity Chapel was the site of Becket's shrine until destroyed in 1538 under Henry VIII. Some thirteenth-century city walls survive and fourteenth-century West Gate, shut even to pilgrims at dusk to keep out robber bands. King's School includes part of the old Benedictine monastery; it has produced many renowned men, including Christopher Marlowe, the Elizabethan playwright, commemorated by the city's Marlowe Theatre, and David Gower, England cricket captain.

Chilham (6m SW of Canterbury): photogenic village on a hill with lovely Tudor and Jacobean cottages and a Jacobean mansion on site of a Norman castle whose keep remains.

Five miles past Folkestone (12m S from Granville, port for ferries to Boulogne) is Hythe, another Cinque Port, with eighteenth-century houses in narrow streets, Martello towers built as defence wall against Napoleon and a dreamy tree-lined canal behind the beach, dug for the same defence. Here begins the world's smallest public railway, running fourteen miles to Dungeness Point, using scale-model steam locos. It passes two old smuggling ports, Dymchurch and New Romney.

Twenty-one miles past Hythe is Rye, superb hillside mediaeval port, with old walls and fourteenth-century gate, narrow cobbled streets, Mermaid Inn (rebuilt 1420, smugglers' headquarters), and Lamb House, home of American author Henry James from 1898–1916.

**Greywalls Hotel
Muirfield, Gullane, East
Lothian, Scotland EH31 2EG
(take A1 E from Edinburgh,
turn onto A198 left or A1 N
from Berwick on Tweed, then
A198 through North Berwick).
Telephone: Gullane (0620)
842144.
DBB E;
SBB B.
Dinner D;
lunch A, B.
Closed December 1–Easter.
No dogs.
Credit cards: Euro, Visa,
Amex, Diners.**

It is not necessary to be a golf enthusiast to enjoy Greywalls, but it helps. This serene house, built in 1901 by Sir Edwin Lutyens, who designed New Delhi and the British Embassy in Washington, is on the very edge of the great Muirfield golf course founded in 1744. If you have never heard of Tom Watson, keep mum. He stayed here and won the British Open, and the championship is due to return in 1986 (book very early). One guest had his bed lined north to south because he believed the magnetic flow improved his golf. There are ten courses within five miles, including a splendid children's course at North Berwick (5m).

Other games have been played here. King Edward VII used to stay to admire the views across the Firth and to the Lammermuir Hills and his mistress Mrs Willy James, wife of the owner. They built him a loo-with-a-view by the garden wall, now a two-room suite ('King's Loo').

I love the house and walled gardens, laid out by the great Edwardian Gertrude Jeckyll. It was the home of the Weaver family until 1948, when they turned it into an hotel. They still live there. The lounging rooms are a delight, especially the library, with big open fire, huge settees, rows of books and interesting pictures. The bar is snug and warm. My bedroom, in a new extension, was perfectly comfortable, had a bathroom big enough to take me and bath towels vast enough to enfold me. Scottish mineral water, heather soap, shampoo, bath oil and even Cologne are provided.

The highly-experienced manageress, Henrietta Ferguson, has a woman's eye for detail and moves silently among her young staff helping them to give a most pleasant, smiling service, so much nicer than slick, unsmiling ritual.

For Royal and Ancient Games.

Food & Drink

Frankly I was a little dubious when I heard that the new chef at Greywalls was only 23. In France he would have expected to have another 10 years experience to be head chef at a place of this standard. But I need not have worried. Andrew Mitchell was assistant to the previous chef, who well deserved his Ronay star, and with a little more experience could reach the heights.

He is inventive and careful. I persuaded neighbours to let me try two of their starters and both were delicious. One was three different French cheeses baked in puff pastry with cider and apple sauce, the other a chilled salmon and halibut terrine wrapped in a dill pancake, with cucumber and mint dressing. But I did think that starters seemed a bit expensive and the set dinner seemed better value. So I chose it.

First course was a really crisp red and green salad with apple, tomatoes and toasted pine kernels, marinaded strips of beef in an orange and almond dressing.

Then came fillet of sea trout fried in butter with prawns and leek, with lemon juice and cream sauce. It was very good indeed. The main course was perfectly-roasted loin of veal coated with shallot and chervil butter, served with pleurote mushrooms (oyster mushrooms which grow on trees and shrubs) in a truffle and tarragon sauce. Good choice of vegetables including delicious French beans and courgettes crispy as fresh cucumber.

The cheeseboard had a fair selection of good fresh cheeses. The dessert was strawberries and pink grapefruit in choux pastry with a cold white chocolate sauce. Coffee and petits fours.

Open Champion Lee Trevino lived on chips. He missed a lot. The wine list includes very funny rhymes by Cyril Ray, funny drawings by Charles Mozley, and some very serious wines. There is a very good choice of cheaper clarets Bourgeois growths, Côtes de Blayes and Bourg – those 'lesser' areas whose wines are fruity when young, a good choice of medium-priced, specialising in Château Cissac, the Haut-Médoc popular in Britain and America, and some great, expensive wines for celebrating a large pools win. The scarcity of half bottles can be restricting. In fact I drank more than I intended with my meal because of this.

A very nice half of Meursault went well with the salad. Luckily I think that red wine, when not too heavy, suits salmon or salmon trout as well as meat, so I took a bottle of a second-growth St Julien claret, Château Leoville-Las-Cases – a little heavy, perhaps, but in my experience always excellent. This was a 1977, slightly lighter than some vintages, with charming flavour. It is a splendid buy.

For lovers of sweet wines for dessert (or, as I like them, very cold for elevenses) this list is strong. It includes glasses, halves, or bottles of Baumes de Venise, that superbly flavoursome Rhône wine, and a choice from Rieussec to Château d'Yquem of Sauternes. Beware, chaps – read first Cyril Ray's warning of how those sweet Bordelaises can get themselves Borderlaide!

The Firth of Forth shore is rich in seabirds. Walk on the long sands or drive to North Berwick (6m) and take a boat to Bass Rock and Fidra (many seabirds, including gannets, shags, razorbills, kittiewakes, fulmars). Aberlady Bay (2m SW of Gullane) has a 1,493-acre nature reserve in sands and dunes, haunt of waders and wildfowl.

Myreton Motor Museum (4m S) has cars, bikes and motorcycles from earliest days and World War II military vehicles. Haddington (6m S) is a charming old town with wide streets and 129 buildings of architectural or historic interest, including a beautiful 1748 Town House by William Adam, father of Robert. A mile on is Lennoxlove House, still home of the Dukes of Hamilton, named after the Duchess of Lennox who modelled the original

Brittania on coins in the seventeenth century. She was called La Belle Stewart. Fine collection of furniture, portraits, porcelain and Royal Stewart souvenirs (open Wednesday, Saturday, Sunday p.m. April–September).

Edinburgh (18m W): one of Europe's most attractive capital cities. Get information, see historical audio-visual narrated by great actor Gordon Jackson, plus six audio-visual tours, at Scottish Experience (W end of Princes St). Buy 1001 Things to See in Scotland (Tourist Board, £1.90) for a good list of Edinburgh's sights. Don't miss the Castle or Holyrood Palace (Royal residence). Superb views of city and Pentland Hills from top of the chairlift at Hillend (S outskirts, Biggar road) above largest artificial ski-slope in Britain.

On A198 E past North Berwick are spectacular ruins

of fourteenth-century
Tantallon Castle, described in
Walter Scott's 'Marmion' –
Douglas stronghold with
100-ft sheer cliffs on three
sides, 'impregnable' until
Cromwell's General Monk
reduced it to ruins in twelve
days in 1651. Continue on A1,
then parallel minor roads

through Spott, Oldhamstocks,
Grantshouse for rewarding
views of coast and
Lammermuir Hills. Back on
A1 at Grantshouse to see
Eyemouth (fishing town with
cobbled streets, archways,
passages, courtyards. N is St
Abbs Head, graveyard of
many ships). On to Berwick-

upon-Tweed (in England –
charming port with a walk
along top of Elizabethan
walls; huge Saturday market.
Three bridges across Tweed.
Salmon netting in season.
Violent history of Anglo-
Scottish warring. Now
Berwick football club plays in
Scottish League).

**Hackness Grange
Country Hotel
North York Moors National
Park, Nr Scarborough,
Yorkshire YO13 0JW.
Telephone: Scarborough
(0723) 69966.
DBB C-D;
SBB A-B;
dinner BB per person B; many
cut-price short breaks.
Dinner (4 course) B;
lunch card from A.
Open all year.
Credit cards: Euro, Visa,
Amex, Diners.**

The North York Moors have wild beauty. Hackness Grange is a near-perfect hideout from which to explore them, with the option of a little night life in the resort of Scarborough five miles away – theatre, dancing, discos. I would stay just to enjoy the view from the bar-lounge. You look across the lawns to the charming trout lake with a pleasant island, lovely trees from maples to thousands of firs and tree-covered high moorland hills beyond. The garden is rich in bird life including different types of duck. It is beautiful in spring, summer sun, autumn colours and under snow in winter. There is a good all-weather tennis court, a big pitch and putt course, eleven miles of private trout fishing on the Derwent and a heated indoor swimming pool with glass walls. A world professional champion, Jack Martin, will teach you casting in the lake.

Very handsome for a mid-Victorian house, the Grange was the dower house of Lord Derwent's family, then the family house of Lord Listowel. I have watched over several years as Ken Hardcastle has turned it from a simple country house hotel into a hospitable, very comfortable three-star hotel – not quite luxurious,

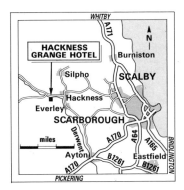

some furnishing banal, but efficient, informal and friendly.

Bedrooms in the main house are light and cheerful, those surrounding a pleasant court-yard with flowers in converted stables are modern and efficient. The upstairs lounge is bright and charming, with more good views.

The staff are friendly – and they stay.

Food & Drink

Old-style Yorkshire cooking, very well accomplished, and with Yorkshire portions. Roast beef red and juicy in the middle, brown outside and crispy skinned, with real Yorkshire pudding. Roast shoulder of pork, the stronger flavoured cut, with apple sauce. Steak and kidney pie. Leg of lamb with mint sauce or homemade redcurrant jelly. Stuffed roast chicken or chicken breast in cream of mushroom sauce. Braised venison in red wine. Grilled steaks, chops, cutlets. Not very inventive, perhaps, but what a joy it is to taste local fresh English meat so well cooked. Vegetables, too, are fresh and mostly local, with some old-fashioned favourites like creamed parsnips, celery in onion sauce, broccoli in cheese sauce. Freshly-baked jacket potatoes are usually among the choices.

This is a great area for game, which is served in season, and even better for fish from rivers and coast. The fish is superb and does not need eccentric 'modern' sauces. It is quite magnificent poached in water, wine or cider. Among the starters at my last dinner were fillet of plaice poached in wine with onion and tomatoes and also a fresh herring salad. Most people chose the ham and cheese pancakes. Next course was sorbet or a super thick homemade vegetable soup. Then came the roasts, grilled steak or poached halibut steak.

There is usually one old-fashioned English steamed pudding among sweets. I was offered also lemon meringue pie, black cherries in kirsch and cream or raspberry cream Norwegian.

I think that it is excellent value. Many guests really do appreciate such good straight cooking, among them Americans, who want to try real English dishes, and German, Dutch and Scandinavian guests.

The wine list is fairly modest, varied and very good value. The dry white house wine is grapey and surprisingly good. It is a clever blend, bottled in Burgundy. I tried a cheap Sauvignon from Bordeaux which was very much to my taste – dry, crisp, slightly acidic, as the French like their wines. One lesser-known white wine is a 1979 Pouilly-Vinzelles – 'Similar to Pouilly-Fuissé,' says the list. Well it's a much earthier wine but I think that the French drink it too young. It gains body in five or six years and can be better than some poorer Pouilly-Fuissé trading on the name. It is also blessedly cheaper. Try this one. It is the right age.

The most expensive wine on the list is a 1973 Château La Lagune third growth red Bordeaux. I regard this as a much under-estimated wine of great smoothness and individual style. In fact, I bought several cases earlier when I could not afford it and have enjoyed every sip of it. Alas, I have only one case left.

Pure Yorkshire

Footpaths to forest trails and into the moors begin in the village. Moor walking can be hilly and quite hard. Hackness, with an eleventh-century church, is the meeting place of five of the few little roads at the eastern, coastal end of the huge National Park, and it is easy to find your way to any of the hamlets in the triangle between Whitby on the coast in the north, Scarborough to the east (of Hackness) and Pickering to the west.

Pickering, charming hilly town with a ruined castle, has a twelfth-century church with murals including Salome dancing for Herod. Pickering is the terminus of the North Yorkshire Moors Railway; it opened in 1863 with horse-drawn carriages and now steam engines pull trains for eighteen miles through lovely scenery to Grosmont, five miles from Whitby. It passes through Goathland, with three spectacular waterfalls – Mallyan Spout, Nellie Ayre Foss and Thomason Foss. A well-preserved stretch of Roman Road can be seen southward.

Whitby was the home of Captain Cook, one of the greatest sailors, explorers and navigators of all time. He started sailing here on colliers, rose from Naval Able Seaman to Captain in nine years. His house in Grape Lane is a small museum. The photogenic old port once had a big whaling fleet; it still has a small fishing fleet. Whitby Abbey was founded in 657AD and the Synod of Whitby was held here when English churches decided to tie up with Rome. The present ruins are from the thirteenth century, partly caused by German naval shelling in 1914. In Bram Stoker's novel, Dracula landed here. Southward, Robin Hood's Bay is one of the most picturesque coastal villages in England, once a haunt of smugglers.

Scarborough, an old fishing village, became a spa in 1622, a bathing resort last century and is still a fishing port; superb freshly landed shellfish can be eaten from stalls by the fishing harbour. Family and action holiday centre – fishing, sailing, parachuting, sub-aqua, flying, and Yorkshire County cricket pitch. Good choice of theatres from musicals to Alan Ayckbourn's Theatre in the Round where all his plays are shown first.

Malton (21m SW of Hackness) – racehorse training centre; old market square around Norman church; markets held Fridays, Saturdays (including livestock).

Castle Howard (5m further W) designed in 1699 for Howard family, who still live there, by Vanburgh, the artist – his first building. Baroque style except one Palladian wing (added later). Painted Hall is brilliant. Paintings include Holbein's Henry VIII.

York (39m from Hackness) – see Middlethorpe Hall, York, page 101.

HOMEWOOD PARK

**Homewood Park Hotel
Hinton Charterhouse, Bath,
Avon BA3 6BB (6m SE of Bath,
just off A36 along lane to
Freshford).
Telephone: Limpley Stoke
(022 122) 2643.
DBB D, E (Continental
breakfast);
SBB C, D; much cheaper
November–March.
Dinner from the card D;
set dinner of fish Thursday
only B;
lunch B.
Closed 2 weeks from
December 24.
No dogs.
Credit cards: Euro, Visa,
Amex, Diners.**

A delightful French friend, normally 'sympathique et correct', scoffs a little at British hotels. I dream sometimes of taking her to stay with Stephen and Penny at Homewood Park. It is one of the best informal family-hotels in Europe.

The Rosses sold their famous Bath restaurant Pobjoys five years ago and moved to this eighteenth-century house enlarged by Victorians and its ten acre park. Here they started a 'restaurant with rooms'. Now it is a fifteen-bedroom hotel. Last winter they added a meticulously-planned extension in the same Bath stone as the original, so that only its fresh

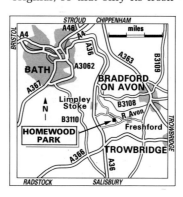

colour betrays it. Inside, the new bedrooms are copies of the old, even to fitted cupboards and wainscotting. And what gentle, welcoming and comfortable bedrooms they are! It is a joy to go to bed at Homewood. But the whole house is the same – decorated and furnished with imagination, taste and thoughtfulness, yet informal. Penny is brilliant at blending soft colours and making spacious rooms with high ceilings seem cosy. A set of prints in the bar-lounge is delightful.

Tennis and croquet in the garden, fine views, a riding school next door, lovely flower beds and fresh flowers around the house, beautiful Bath six miles away, and Stephen Ross's superb cooking ... take someone you love and purr while they admire your taste.

I recommended Homewood in 1981 in my *Travellers' Britain* and now people write to recommend it to us! It is far from cheap, but many hotels not half so heavenly charge far more. And there are winter bargains when log fires burn and game is in season.

Food & Drink

Stephen Ross is a young dedicated master chef, still experimenting and learning. He loves to try something new but has a sound base in British and French traditional cooking. I do not understand how the *Good Food Guide* could have called him 'avowedly French'. True, last time I was at Homewood he offered as a starter squid in Provençal style but an alternative was Cornish pilchards with horseradish cream. Another speciality is Cornish crab tart. He cooks Cornish shark very nicely, too, but is better known for stuffed chicken breasts with watercress purée.

I find his cooking delicious — light but flavoursome, interesting but with none of the excesses of some cooks striving desperately to be 'modern'. Some of his specialities are leek, chive and yoghurt soup, which is thick yet delicate, wild rabbit sausage served with a creamy garlic sauce, which is very tasty, sweetbread, prawn and saffron tart, and a tasty soufflé of Roquefort cheese and walnut. But perhaps the favourite is his saddle of venison with orange and Grand Marnier sauce.

I can recommend his grapefruit and Campari sorbet, though normally I regard Campari as a mouth wash rather than a drink. (Would it mix with grapefruit juice?) Traditionalists go for his splendid rum and orange bread and butter pudding. Vegetables are often fresh from the garden and perfectly cooked. The plates and dishes are of Wedgwood, the service efficient and friendly, the high-ceilinged dining room spacious and with generous gaps between tables.

The wine list is sensible, well balanced and fairly strong in Rhône red and Loire white. House wines are varied and cheap.

I tried a Pouilly-Fumé Les Loges, still one of the best and good value. Try it with that crab tart or the leek, chive and yoghurt soup. There is also an interesting 1982 Savanières from the famous Madame Joly's vineyards La Roche aux Moines. This is one of the two Grand Cru wines of the Anjou Loire – but a little young and crude. It could have done with two more years. A good list of white Burgundies includes a 1982 Rully from the admirable Domaine de la Folie – a crisp wine, and a Chablis Montée de Tonnerre 1983 from Jean Durup – one of the best Premier Cru wines.

But I settled last time for a rarer white, a 1981 St Joseph from Jean-Louis Grippat at Tournon. St Joseph faces Hermitage across the Rhône and has similar rocky slopes. For reds, I would pick the strong, tasty, heavy Gigondas 1980 to accompany heavier dishes like venison and beef; for lighter dishes a 1976 Château de la Rivière Fronsac at slightly more. This lesser known Bordeaux area produces fine tasting wines with freshness, which develop nicely after six–eight years.

Homewood wines are very good value.

Bath – the essence of elegance in its streets and crescents of fine buildings in honey-coloured stone. Its hot springs, discovered by the Romans, gush a quarter million gallons of water daily at a temperature of 49°C (120°F). From early 1600s Royal visitors went there for cures but it was in 1703 that Beau Nash, professional gambler and arbiter of extravagant fashion, became Master of Ceremonies and inspired the Assembly and Pump rooms. Yorkshire architects John Wood, father and son, used honey-coloured local stone to build in the neoclassical style of Palladio, the Italian from Vicenza.

There is much to see and you must walk to see it properly. Do not miss Royal Crescent, Pulteney Bridge with shops on each side like Florence's Ponte Vecchio, or Queen Square, the Woods' first masterpiece, where Jane Austen and Wordsworth lived. Try to see Lilliput Alley, where Sally Lunn sold her famous Bath buns; the world's largest costume museum beautifully displayed in the Assembly

Rooms, rebuilt after wartime bombing; the carriage museum in Circus Mews, and the Holbourne museum in an eighteenth-century house with a fine collection of silver, porcelain, glass and paintings by Reynolds, Gainsborough and Stubbs.

Claverton Manor, 3m E of Bath, is the American Museum in Britain, showing American domestic life in seventeenth–nineteenth centuries, with furniture, household equipment and period rooms.

Dyrham Park (8m N of Bath) is a pleasant manor house (built 1692–1702) in a delightful park. A Tudor house was altered and refaced in two styles – the first formal and symmetric; the second, East, front by William Talman more ornate with Italian Baroque orangery. Inside is a fine collection of Delft ware, Flemish tapestries, and paintings including Murillo's 'Peasant Woman and Boy'. National Trust.

Chipping Sodbury (15m N of Bath) is charming market town. See also Burleigh Court Hotel page 27.

Our choice in an area bulging with fine hotels.

HOPE END

Hope End Hotel
Hope End, near Ledbury,
Hereford and Worcester
HR8 1DS
(from Ledbury take B4214
under railway bridge, take
right to Wellington Heath; 2m
on bear right to hotel).
Telephone: Ledbury (0531)
3613.
Dinner, bed and breakfast
only B per person.
Dinner C (5 courses).
Closed last weekend of
November to last weekend of
February.
No children under 12.
Credit cards: Euro, Visa,
Amex, Diners.

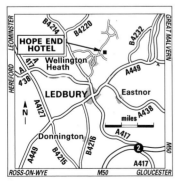

How nice to have your hunches justified! I went to Hope End some years ago when seeking for a TV programme the Turkish folly with minarets where Elizabeth Barrett spent twenty-three happy years before her eccentric and financially-unstable father moved her to Wimpole Street – from where she eloped with Robert Browning. I found only one minaret, a massive archway, iron gates and the original pretty Queen Anne house which her father had enveloped with Eastern extravagance. And there were Patricia Hegarty, a teacher who had inherited it, and her husband John, a solicitor, making it into a home and hotel. 'What a nice and unusual hotel it will make,' I said, and we put it on TV.

Already she had a formidable herb garden, an acre of walled vegetable garden, fruit trees and bushes, and bantams and goats, all in forty acres of pasture and woods with an overgrown lake rich in waterbirds. And already decor and furnishings were in plain, sealed wood, from loo seats to tables. Bedrooms have since been made more comfortable and there are new ones under the minaret and in a cottage in the grounds. A charming lounge is on the first floor, large and light with six comfortable settees; a smaller one is downstairs. There are books everywhere, but no TV anywhere. Perhaps they did not like our programme.

Food&Drink

Patricia Hegarty cooks a five course set meal, changed each day. She tries to use organically produced ingredients and cooks only locally produced meat, fish and game, serving fruit, herbs and vegetables from her own garden, eggs from her own poultry and milk for beautiful yoghurt from her own goats.

The brown bread is freshly baked. Her vegetables are freshly picked or dug and she makes superb fresh salads of great variety. It is healthy cooking without faddiness, and nostalgic, for it brings back

tastes of our childhood, when the main 'convenience' foods were baked beans and corned beef and chickens were free to cross the road. Many of her dishes go back much further than that. Fillet of Wye pike is served with lemon butter sauce. As our sweet we had elderflower and gooseberry cream. And she hunts out English and Welsh cheeses few people know. Our choice was Cornish pepper cheese and Shorthorn blue Cheshire.

We started with a delicious tomato and rosemary soup, and a soufflé of lovage. She also uses this old herb for soups. We grew it in our herb bed and did

not know what it was for a long time. It has a spicy flavour – for me, lemon with a dash of curry. Known in the old days as the All Healing Plant, it was used for cleansing the system and as an antiseptic on wounds. The Romans brought it over for scenting their baths. Pubs here once sold it as a cordial. In soup it is usually cooked and creamed with potatoes and leeks, then cream added.

The main course was Hereford beef in mustard and savoury sauce, with broad beans, new young carrots and steamed new potatoes. The salad was lettuce and baby courgette.

You can have coffee, Indian tea or a choice of China teas. The hotel's own spring water is served, too – the Malvern Water Mrs Thatcher has been plugging.

John's wine list is extensive and well chosen, with a choice of more than 100 bottles and fifty half bottles.

For a bargain red with meat, poultry and cheese I would go for the 1975 Château Vrai Canon Bouché. These Canon Fronsac clarets have a charming fresh flavour which they keep with maturity while losing their sharp tannic edge. For a much dearer choice, the 1970 Brane-Cantenac Margaux, second growth, is one of the great years of one of the fine wines of Bordeaux. It makes me thirsty to think about it!

A very drinkable cheap Burgundy red is a first growth Fixin (pronounced Fissin) from Pierre Gelin's Clos Napoleon (formerly Aux Cheusots). It is not quite of Gevrey-Chambertin standard (or price) but is above the run of most rustic wines from here, is a lovely dark colour and is maturing slowly but well.

For a white, there is no need to go further than a genuine Marcel Vincent Château de Fuissé Pouilly-Fuissé 1981 at a remarkably low price for this wine. Grab it, before I go back and drink John dry of it.

For possibly a new experience, try the white Rhône Condrieu by the local King of Winemakers, Georges Vernay – unusual and rare wine from a rare Viognier grape grown on steep slopes of decomposed rock which annoyingly keeps washing back into the valley.

A fruity Muscadet (Gillières) served by the glass, half or full bottle is a good aperitif.

There is one organically-grown Provence red on the list. I have not tried it and wonder how it survives the competition with Fronsac and Fixin.

Ledbury is a lovable little town with a market supported on wooden pillars, half timbered houses and seven historic inns, so historic research is rewarding. Narrow Church Lane is unchanged since Tudor days. In the wide main street a battle was fought between Cromwell's soldiers and the mounted Cavaliers led by the ostentatious Prince Rupert of the Rhine. For once, the Royalists won.

Beyond are the Malvern Hills, nine miles long. In attractive scenery are Malvern Wells, which supply Malvern water and where you can still take the Waters at the Holy Well. Great Malvern (8m from Ledbury) is an interesting Victorian town on hillsides where, under old Common rights, sheep are allowed to graze on grass beside the avenue. It is expensive to run one down. Malvern put on George Bernard Shaw's plays when others would not, and the Shaw Festival is now revived. Elgar, the composer, lived at Malvern Wells. Jenny Lind, the 'Swedish Nightingale', lived and is buried here. Morgan sports cars are still hand-made here, partly of wood. This is hop and fruit country.

Worcester (8m past Great Malvern) is an ancient city on the banks of the river Severn. Rich in old buildings, it is compact enough to walk round. The cathedral was started in 1087, has a lovely crypt and a fourteenth-century tower. The tomb of King John, the brother of Richard Lionheart (forced by the Barons to sign the Magna Carta of freedom for the Barons!), includes an effigy of his face. The cathedral overlooks the beautiful and peaceful Worcester county cricket ground. The Royal Worcester Porcelain Works can be visited by appointment; it was started in 1751.

See also Pengethley Hotel, Ross-on-Wye, page 114.

Elizabeth Barrett Browning lived here.

KENNEL HOLT

Kennel Holt
Cranbrook, Kent, TN17 2PT
(2 miles from Cranbrook off
A262 from Goudhurst).
Telephone: (0580) 712032.
Dinner, bed and breakfast
(according to room and
season): single B; double D–E
(price includes afternoon tea,
dinner, coffee, room, morning
tea, paper, breakfast and
service).
Menu (set dinner) B;
snack lunch or picnic A.
Closed December 23–
January 26.
Credit cards in non-residents'
restaurant only.
No children under age 6; high
tea provided.
Reductions for children
sharing parents' room.
Dogs by arrangement.

Kennel Holt is a superb place to hide away with someone you love – only fifty miles from London.

It is in the glorious Weald of Kent, a lush land of rolling hills and winding valleys with little streams, all patterned with fruit orchards, corn fields, rich green pastures with plump sheep and lambs, woodlands hiding rarer birds and wild animals and hop gardens flanked by round and square kilns. Webs of little lanes and secretive roads join hamlets and villages. Timbered black-and-white Tudor cottages and farmhouses and old white clapboard houses outnumber modern bungalows.

Kennel Holt is in a valley hidden from any road. You reach it along a 300-yard private lane under trees – an Elizabethan manor with later additions in five acres of lawns with duck pond, vegetable garden, and tree-lined paths. Inside, it is beamed, spacious and comfortable, with a roomy entrance hall, two lounges with open fires, a cosy, intimate dining room for hotel residents and a

separate pleasant restaurant for those who come to dinner.

Bedrooms are thoughtfully and comfortably furnished with antiques. There are only seven rooms, so book early. All have bathroom, radio, colour TV and hairdryer. Patrick Cliff and his wife Ruth, former teacher at a resident Cordon Bleu cookery school, have been there only three years. The hotel has never been so good.

It has just been accepted by the French-run Relais du Silence organization, promising quiet, peace and rest. I am not surprised.

The dining room setting at Kennel Holt is a joy – gleaming silver, sparkling cut-glass rich-coloured cloths and real damask napkins, candles friendliness, food well served But you will not get much choice – just a menu of five courses, with choices of mair dishes and desserts. Nor wil you get complicated or unusua dishes. In this area almos

everything is produced nearby, and what you need is meticulous cooking and appropriate sauces – not innovation. That is what Ruth Cliff provides.

The menu at my last dinner was a pleasant hors d'oeuvre, a really nice soup from local mushrooms, and a main course choice of Dover sole meunière or saddle of hare, served with a cream sauce and grapes. There were plenty of good fresh vegetables cooked with exactness, followed by cheese (real farmhouse cheddar or Stilton) and a fair choice of desserts from an old English style boiled pudding to light confections with fresh fruit.

You get a real old English cooked breakfast with lots of choice, including local free-range eggs and famous Kent sausages.

The set dinner-time of 8 o'clock worries me. This is done to ensure that everything is freshly cooked and served. As a late eater, I tend to sit drinking more wine if I have to eat earlier. Happily the Kennel Holt wine list is one of the cheapest I have found in good British hotels.

In summer 1985 the red, white and rosé housewines cost £3.95 a bottle. I have not tried the rosé, but the dry white Blanc de Blancs was excellent

value. Though shipped from Chablis, it is probably made from Sauvignon grapes rather than the Chardonnay used for Chablis itself. Some very drinkable Sauvignon wines are made in the Yonne département. The red, shipped from the Rhône is surprisingly smooth and heavy. A real premier cru Fourchaume Chablis from Defert cost us only £9.95. Another time we had a good Sancerre, with plenty of grape taste, from Domaine les Groux for £7.70. Among reds, there is a remarkable bargain at just over £10 – a Varoilles Gevrey Chambertin 1980 which is delightfully mellow and equal to most Grand Cru wines.

One of the very best of Beaujolais, a Brouilly from Château de la Chaize, was good value. There is also a tempting list of bin-ends. You might find even greater value among these. Definitely an hotel for keen wine consumers. Make sure your partner is, too.

The Weald is rich in lovely scenery, attractive villages and little towns, and has enormous historic interest, yet it is little known to tourists. It is an area for explorers and wanderers.

Cranbrook (2m) has a high street of old white board houses and shops, a fine mediaeval church and a superb white board windmill in sail. Two miles on are the beautiful gardens of Sissinghurst Castle, laid out by Sir Harold Nicolson and his wife the writer Victoria Sackville-West partly in Elizabethan style; they also rescued part of the derelict old house. You can visit the sixteenth-century tower where she wrote her books. Two miles west are more gardens at Glassenbury Park, a moated eighteenth-century manor. The horse Napoleon rode at Waterloo is buried here.

Goudhurst (3m NW of Cranbrook) – a photogenic, hillside village, its main street lined with old houses and shops rising from the duck pond and the Vine inn to the thirteenth- to fifteenth-century church, white Weavers' Hall, and mediaeval Star and Eagle Inn. The inn, a former monastery, became headquarters of the Hawkhurst smuggling gang who brought their loot from Romney marshes by mule and terrorised half of Kent. Finchcocks, lovely old house, is a music museum.

Quiet, peace, rest in Kent's glorious countryside.

At Horsmonden, three miles from Goudhurst, a woodland walk goes to Furnace Pond where the guns were cooled. You can sit in the Gun Inn where the great seventeenth-century gunmaker John Browne designed guns with impartiality for Charles I and Cromwell, the British Navy and its Dutch enemy, beside the same inglenook where huge joints still cook over apple logs. Between Horsmonden and Tonbridge (10m) is Tudeley village church with superb modern stained glass windows by Marc Chagall who designed the modern windows in Rheims cathedral; he finished the Tudeley glass just before his death in 1985.

Kennel Holt is twelve miles from one of our most elegant towns, Royal Tunbridge Wells – a rival to Bath as a spa in Regency days. The Regency meeting place, the Pantiles, is still there, and so are elegant Regency parades and hundreds of houses designed by Decimus Burton.

Beyond Tunbridge Wells (6¾m NW) is the pretty village of Penshurst and Penshurst Place, fourteenth-century manor house with an Elizabethan front, standing in magnificent parkland on the rivers Eden and Medway. Here Sir Philip Sidney – poet, courtier, statesman and courageous soldier – was born in 1554 and one of his descendants, Viscount de l'Isle, VC, lives today. The state rooms, including the superb Great Hall dating from 1340, and a toy museum are open from April–October.

Rye, the ancient Cinque Port, is 20 miles. Leeds Castle (16m NE near M20) is one of the loveliest castles in the world. Moated and mediaeval, it has fine collections of furniture, pictures – and dog collars! (Open April–October)

Kirkby Fleetham

**Kirkby Fleetham Hall
Kirkby Fleetham,
Northallerton,
North Yorkshire DL7 0SU
(take A684 signposted to
Northallerton off A1 north of
turnings to Thirsk and Ripon;
left to Kirkby Fleetham
village. Hotel 1m on).
Telephone: Northallerton
(0609) 748226.
DBB C–D;
SBB B.
Dinner B.
Open all year.
Credit cards: Visa, Amex,
Diners.**

This historic and lovely country mansion, dating from 1600 and enlarged at the end of the seventeenth century, might be an abandoned ruin but for the courage and hard work of David Grant, former marketing man with Unilever, and his wife Chris, computer feeder. The two wings were abandoned, the rest run down, the garden a wilderness when they bought it in 1980. They have returned it to its former glory, added a modern bathroom to each bedroom, furnished it with fine antiques, and redecorated with their own hands the whole of this vast house, with huge rooms and high ceilings. You will see what a task that has been if you look at the ornate ceiling of the coffee lounge, decorated in two colours by Chris.

Now they have restored the gardens and thirty acre park, too, with lake, flower beds and lawn. To lay out this park in 1740, the owner had the village knocked down and rebuilt a mile away. The twelfth-century church remains beside the Hall, with a memorial to a

former estate owner, a Knight Templar, who died in 1290. David Grant now has the right to be buried in the church and to read the lesson, though he does not have time for either at present.

The house is delightfully furnished and has a relaxing but by no means dead atmosphere. The front terrace looks across lawns to a huge bank of daffodils below a wood. The superb dining room, with mahogany tables and fine old chairs, looks to the lake. You dine by candlelight off Wedgwood china and drink from fine crystal glass. There is no bar. Drinks are kept in a huge antique wardrobe in a charming lounge with open fire. Most bedrooms are spacious enough to be bed-sitters.

The surrounding countryside, a mile from the roaring A1, is laced with narrow lanes, a few hamlets and little traffic, as you might expect of what is now called the 'Herriot Country' in honour of the superb vet books by James Herriot.

Food & Drink

Chris Grant believes in variety, and has the courage to experiment. She changes every choice on the menu daily, uses the best fresh ingredients she can find, cooks them all fresh. I love her cooking. It is basically English, nicely filling without being heavy.

She makes some splendid soups, served first in the British manner, before the pâté and such. I had a delicious tomato and basil soup recently, with sharp tomato flavour, not killed by sugar and cream. Her old-fashioned, genuine beef consommé with sherry is prized, too. Some of her next courses are less British – like melon with grape sorbet, baked banana in puff pastry with curry mayonnaise, but she also makes a good egg and ham mousse.

Pork fillets with apple, raisins, cream and Calvados, fresh salmon baked in wine with beurre blanc, saddle of hare, lamb steak with rosemary sauce, are typical of her main courses. Her vegetables are a joy – fresh seasonal, tasting as if they have just come from the garden. Her sweets are mostly light and fruity. A choice of cheeses follows.

A much-travelled American said that it was the best value for money he could remember eating in Britain.

The wine list is incredible. David says: 'We have always collected wines like other people collect stamps.' He brought his collection here. His list gives a useful guide to the weight and dryness of wines from many areas, and a description of their qualities. There are plenty of lower- and middle-priced wines on the list and the prices of the older, greater wines are below the current market price – some way below. I cannot read the claret list without drooling. But it is a fine opportunity to increase your knowledge of wines by trying, for instance, a cheap Chenas, little known Beaujolais of which little is produced, good red and white Rully Burgundy (some winesmen seek the white to replace ordinary Chablis, which is becoming overpriced and sometimes mediocre), a 1975 Richebourg red Burgundy, beloved by our grandfathers but not seen much in Britain now (and not cheap, either), or a Bollinger red still wine from the Champagne, rarer even than Bouzy. Plenty of half bottles for 'tastings' including a Châteaux Margaux.

Do not hesitate to ask David Grant to recommend a wine in your price range for the meal you choose. He knows his wines well and is justly proud of them. This is a great hotel in which to spend a week or two with a partner who has a thirst for wine.

LOCAL DRIVES The Vale of York begins here, between the wild North York Moors and the huge Dales National Park with Pennine Peaks and the great valleys of Wharfedale and Swaledale carved by huge glaciers a million years ago. Follow the minor roads and you will find scenic treasures everywhere. Little market towns, too – Northallerton (6m E – cobbled verges, market cross, partly-mediaeval inn); Thirsk (14m SE – old market town with racecourse, famous inn Golden Fleece and now known as the place where James Herriot and Helen lived at Skeldale House in the vet series); Helmsley (29m SE on North York Moors, with restored old buildings and market on Friday; Rievaulx Abbey is a huge ghostly ruin of twelfth-century abbey built by French monks); Bedale (just across A1, W on A684 – Georgian town with market held since thirteenth century, church guarded by portcullis, and Bedale Hall, Georgian house with superb ballroom and a museum). Past Bedale (8m) are ruins of twelfth-century Jervaulx Abbey, dissolved by Henry VIII. Richmond (across A1 9m N of Bedale) is dramatically placed overlooking the river Swale – a lovely old town with huge eleventh-century castle in romantic ruin, many fine old buildings, big cobbled market place (Saturday market) and tiny narrow streets. Ripon (18m S) is a fine old town with superb cathedral, started in the twelfth century. Beyond are the beautiful ruins of Fountains Abbey, once the wealthiest in England because the monks were in the wool trade.

The hotel recommends six very good easy day drives.

For Harrogate, York (38m) and Harewood House, see Middlethorpe Hotel, York, page 101.

Stay with a Lord of the Manor, who collects wines.

Knockinaam Lodge

Knockinaam Lodge Hotel
Portpatrick,
Wigtownshire, Scotland
DG9 9AD
(on west coast of the Mull of
Galloway, 3m from
Portpatrick village; 7m from
ferry port of Stranraer).
Telephone: Portpatrick (077
681) 471.
Dinner, bed and breakfast
only A–C per person
(seasonal).
Dinner C, 5 courses
(supplements for some dishes,
such as lobster).
Closed early January–Easter.
Credit cards: Visa, Amex,
Diners (not Euro).

A dream-place for a relaxed, informal holiday with friendly service, delightful cooking, fine wines and superb sea views, sometimes to the Irish coast. It is in thirty acres at the foot of a deep wooded glen, with cliffs on three sides – so secluded that Churchill could use it for a secret meeting with Eisenhower and their Chiefs of Staff in the Second World War. A lovely garden has wide lawns running down to a private sandy beach.

From many rooms you can watch the changing moods of the sea and vivid sunsets.

The Lodge was built in 1869 as a holiday home for Lady Hunter-Blair, whose family had owned much of the Mull of Galloway for two centuries. A French chef turned it into a restaurant with rooms in 1971 and around six years ago it was made into an hotel by Simon Pilkington, master of wine, and his wife Caroline. They are improving it all the time, especially the bedrooms, which are centrally heated now – though our bedroom still had an electric blanket. Two comfortable lounges have lots of books, magazines and interesting original paintings, some by local artists.

Simon and Caroline did have their heart set on a bigger place a little nearer to the fleshpots in 1985. Happily for us they were gazumped and now they have decided to stay. I shall try to work my way through a bit more of their excellent wine cellar soon – just in case they do go and take the wine with them!

Complete relaxation with fine food and wisely-picked wines

Food & Drink

For the food and wine alone, I would choose to stay here. Chef John Henry cooks with skill and imagination but respects tradition and wisely restricts the number of dishes to ensure care and freshness. As he also has the wonderful raw materials that this part of Scotland provides liberally from its hills, pastures, forests, streams and fishing villages, eating here is very rewarding.

With tender Galloway beef always available, local lobster, scallops and scampi, wild salmon in season, and superb white fish, especially sole, it would be near to sacrilege to smother them with 'inventive' sauces for the sake of it. John Henry knows better. But he does have a nice ginger sauce for poached salmon if you want it, will top fillet steak with his own liver pâté and Madeira sauce or serve it with a sauce of port and mustard. He also serves luscious fillets of sole filled with salmon mousse, poached in white wine and finished with cream. And he can offer an unusual sauce for grilled lamb cutlets – redcurrant, flavoured with gin, which I assure you is more exciting than Nouvelle's perpetual raspberry vinegar. But mostly he saves his personal touches for starters – such as prawns in strawberry sauce, served hot in a pastry case.

He serves soup as one course each evening. His carrot and orange soup is praised, and Barbara says that his mushroom soup is possibly the best she has had.

You might expect, from a Master of Wine, a wine list as long as *Gone With the Wind* containing dozens of magnificent but frustratingly expensive great clarets and Burgundies. Simon Pilkington must have been talking to my bank manager. The result is a beautifully-chosen list of youngish clarets, ready to drink, and some good dearer Burgundies, but nowhere near the millionaires-only class.

Of the clarets, the dearest is possibly the best, Leoville Poy-ferré 1979, a second-growth not in the same class as Leoville-Las-Cases these days, but with a blend of fruit and tannin which makes it pleasant drinking now. Château Potensac from Lower Médoc is a reliable wine and the 1975 should be just about right. I would have thought that the 1979 Croizet-Bages had time to improve but Simon Pilkington knows more than I do. Ask him about the cheaper wines, including Crus Bourgeois. They would not be here unless they were good in their class.

Among the Burgundies, the 1970 Grands Echézeaux is a gorgeous full and rich wine. Roger's Burgundy shippers, Chanson, own Les Fèves, so if you are in a mood to knock back a magnum, here it is – 1970 Clos des Fèves, one of the top Premiers Crus from Beaune.

To drink with her lobster, Barbara found herself a nice fruity cheap white Sancerre to her taste, Le Grand Chemarin. Quite a relief – she did not notice a superb, subtle Corton-Charlemagne white Burgundy at three times the price!

Portpatrick was the main port between Scotland and Northern Ireland in the days of sail and early steam and you can see the ruins of a seventeenth-century church in which the ministers married eloping couples for £10. Most came from Ireland – officers and gentlemen running away with heiresses before father could catch them.

Later the ferry was transferred to Stranraer, more protected (4m NE); from there, ferries still run to Larne.

Logan Botanic Gardens (12m S) are packed with exotic trees from China, South America and Australia and have avenues of Chusan and cabbage palms. Nearby at Port Logan is a curious tidal fish-pond in rocks, cut in 1800 to provide fish for the kitchens of Logan House, but the fish were treated as family pets. Tame cod still come to be fed by hand. Open in summer.

The actual Mull of Galloway at the southern tip is a wild, narrow peninsula ringed by steep cliffs of multi-coloured rock; thousands of seabirds in summer.

At Glenluce (12m E of Portpatrick) is Lochinch Castle with gardens between two lochs, inspired by Versailles; also ruins of Glenluce Abbey 2m NW of village. Take the small road to New Luce and on to Barrhill. This crosses hilly moorland beside the Waters of Luce, with fine views. At Barrhill

take A714 to Bargrennan (real old Scots country inn used by fishermen 'House o' Hill' with salmon and trout fishing on river Cree). Follow a small road to Glentrool village, then a signposted lane to Loch Trool.

You are in the key spot of seven fir forests covering 130,000 acres of what were bare mountain, stripped by previous landlords, until the Forestry Commission replanted. On a hilltop you will see Bruce's Stone, a memorial to Robert Bruce whose men ambushed English soldiers across the Loch on the opposite hillside, and rolled stones on them. That was in 1306. The view is lovely down to the loch and to green and mauve hills. On the loch behind trees is a secluded mansion which belongs to the Littlewood family – the biggest pools' winners of all.

Marked hill walks start by Bruce's Stone. Foresters ask you to leave your name, the path you intend to take and expected return time. Mishaps are possible, even to us! Rescuers need information. The hills, streams and forests are rich in rarer birds, fox, deer, red squirrel, otter and wild goat. Continue S on A714 to Newton Stewart. This town on the River Cree has pleasant shops and inns and a mill making mohair cloth.

Eastwards, by the coast or the road around Loch Ken to Dumfries, is attractive and interesting country. See Balcary Bay Hotel, page 4.

LAINSTON HOUSE

Lainston House
Sparsholt, Winchester,
Hampshire SO21 2LT
(3m NW of Winchester just off
A272).
Telephone: Winchester (0962)
63588.
DBB E–F; luxury suite F;
SBB C.
Dinner card around D;
lunch B.
Open all year.
Credit cards: Euro, Visa,
Amex, Diners.

The taste of this truly-handsome William and Mary-period red brick house grows stronger and stronger for me. It is expensive for a country hotel, but worth every pound if you have it. It reveals new treasures for me each day. The house has been beautifully and painstakingly restored, from the cornices and wooden panelling to the magnificent oak and mahogany staircase, the original hall fireplace surrounded by eighteenth-century Delft tiles, and the ornamental gardens. The Cedar Room bar is panelled from a tree toppled in the grounds by a storm in 1930. The green dining room is delightful – bright, warm-looking and commanding a view of the flower beds.

The bedrooms vary considerably in size, hence price differences. All have good bathrooms. The smaller ones are under the eaves, comfortable and well furnished. Others are enormous, elegant and beautifully furnished in period style. Some of the loveliest are on the ground floor of the Chudleigh Wing,

with French windows direct to the 65-acre grounds. I slept recently in a huge, delicious room there, all alone and dreaming that the naughty Elizabeth Chudleigh would return. She came to Lainston as a girl of sixteen in the 1760s and became maid-of-honour to Augusta, Princess of Wales. In secret, by night in Lainston chapel, she married the naval officer grandson of the Earl of Bristol. He went to sea, she became the mistress of the Duke of Kingston, then married him bigamously. The scandal caused Parliament to invent the reading of Banns of Marriage and Elizabeth to go to Moscow, where she delighted the court of Catherine the Great by starting a brandy distillery. I raise a glass to her portrait in the hall.

Lainston's special atmosphere arises from the sheer enthusiasm of the owner, Richard Fannon. He came as manager in 1983 from La Toc Hotel in St Lucia, fell in love with Lainston, took over in 1984 and still loves it.

Food & Drink

Chef Friedrich Litty is German-born but used to work in London's Swiss Centre and there are some Swiss touches in his dishes and some of his own. With the beef consommé he serves small choux buns filled with liver parfait – Swiss. With Ogen melon he serves an apricot and Madeira sorbet – his own idea and very good. He is also fond of serving fondant and lyonnaise potatoes.

For a starter I chose a pancake filled with herbs, spinach and a clever blend of cheeses. If choosing fish, I would be tempted by the grilled Hampshire trout, for there are some fine trout rivers around here. But the chef's speciality, much praised, is a mousseline of sole, brill, lobster and spinach with prawn and white wine sauce. Two main course specialities are almost equally delicious: strips of veal cooked to perfection in a wild mushroom and white wine sauce with buttered noodles, and medallions of beef flamed in vodka in a fresh thyme and rosemary sauce finished with sour cream. I have long believed that rosemary goes as well with beef as with lamb.

Friedrich Litty's cooking is thoughtful and careful and his dishes uniformly good. After such a fine meal it seems a little mean to say that I would like to see the dinner price reduced by two or three pounds. That would bring this fine food within range of many gastronomes with less to spend. Both lunches, with less choice and simpler dishes, are good value and there is a two course cheap lunch of soup, buffet and a glass of wine.

Wine prices are far from the top – better value than most equivalent hotels, except perhaps the great first growth clarets, Latour and Mouton-Rothschild, which are way outside my range, anyway. For any of the meat dishes you could choose the Chianti Classico Antinori, one of the two best Chiantis, at under £10. Or there is a Château du Cauze Grand Cru St Emilion for a little more.

If you like white Beaujolais, there is a good 1978 Louis Jadot here. I don't really like the weight with the flavour, and would go for Chablis Vaillons from Domaine La Jouchère – an outstanding first growth of which the 1982 on this list should be drunk, I think, before 1987 at the latest to keep its definite flavour.

There are a dozen or so half bottles.

 You start with a one mile drive through the 65-acre grounds to reach the big front gate. There are views of the Downs, which make fine walking country, and the hotel is a good centre for sightseeing or doing business in Winchester, superlative old city but real traffic problems, or even Southampton (12m S).

Winchester, a Roman city, was made capital of Saxon England by King Alfred in the ninth century and stayed so for 200 years. The 556ft long cathedral started in 1079, was finished in 1404. Treasures include memorial window to 'Compleat Angler' Izaak Walton, a black marble

Norman font, seven eleborately-carved chancery chapels for special masses, mediaeval wall paintings, and the splendid tombs of ancient kings, including Canute; in the library, a thirteenth-century Bible and tenth-century history by Bede. St Swithin asked in AD862 to be buried in the churchyard where rain would fall on him. They moved him inside in 971 and now if it rains on July 15, his day, we get forty days' rain, especially if there are Test Matches on. Two original city gates survive and fine houses from thirteenth-century to Georgian. Winchester College, founded 1382, is one of our oldest schools.

Romsey (10m SW) is on the river Test, one of Britain's best trout and salmon rivers; market town built round tenth-century abbey, sold when Henry VIII dissolved the monasteries. Twelfth-century church remains. Broadlands House, built by John Holland and Capability Brown, was home of Lord Palmerston, Queen Victoria's acid and brilliant Foreign Minister who achieved friendship with the French after centuries of wars and was called 'the Devil's Son' by the Germans, and Earl Mountbatten of Burma, wartime naval hero, Far East Commander, Viceroy of India,

murdered later by Irish Republican terrorists. He was an uncle of Prince Philip and the Queen and Prince spent part of their honeymoon here; so did Prince Charles and Diana. Open to the public. Lord Romsey, Mountbatten's heir, lives there. See also Chewton Glen Hotel, page 34.

Stockbridge (6m NW of Sparsholt) has some of the world's best trout fishing in the River Test. Further on are Salisbury, then the megaliths of Stonehenge (Bronze Age, still mystifying modern historians). Salisbury Cathedral, delicate and dramatic, is one of Europe's loveliest buildings. Started in 1220, it was finished in 1258, while the spire was added in 1334. The Purbeck stone columns inside are superbly dramatic. Old houses in the Close include thirteenth-century Bishop's Palace and beautifully decorated eighteenth-century Mompesson House. Only foundations remain of Old Sarum, Roman fort and original city. See also Bishopstrow House Hall, page 17. Old Sarum was the most notorious rotten borough. Ten electors returned two MPs to Parliament. Abolished by 1832 Reform Act. William Pitt the Elder (1708–78) was a member for Old Sarum and became prime minister.

Elegant abode of an errant Duchess.

Lamorna Cove

Lamorna Cove Hotel
Lamorna Cove, Nr Penzance,
Cornwall TR19 6XH (on south
coast of the 'toe' of Cornwall
just off B3315 between
Penzance – 5m – and Land's
End).
Telephone: Penzance (0736)
731411.
DBB CD;
SBB AB;
dinner, bed and breakfast AB
per person.
Dinner A;
lunch A.
Closed end-November to mid-
February.
Credit cards: Euro, Visa,
Amex, Diners.

There is such a higgledy-piggledy mixture of architectural periods that this highly-regarded hotel, above a lovely protected cove in sunny South Cornwall, could have been a disaster. In fact it has charm, character and is excellent value, especially if you book dinner, bed and breakfast terms.

Snuggling in five acres of thick flowers, trees and shrubs on the slopes of Lamorna Valley, it has an idyllic setting, with views over the valley and to sea over a cove to the distant Lizard Point. It takes five minutes to walk down to the sea – and twenty minutes up again!

Originally a hostel for stone quarry workers, and the owner's house with its own private chapel, it was converted by the Bolton family without losing its character. A modern white building joined to the old stone buildings contains bedrooms and a fine light dining room with one wall of bare granite. Bungalows in the grounds have more bedrooms, excellent for families.

There are many fine antiques, though some bedrooms have modern furnishings. Lamorna has always lured artists, including Munnings, Stanhope Forbes, Dame Laura and Harold Knight, and many slightly lesser known, and there are original paintings around the hotel, including a well-known painting of the cove by the local artist Lamorna Birch RA.

The sheltered, attractive heated swimming pool has a terrace with superb sea views. All bedrooms have good sea or valley views, though they vary in size. There is a sauna and solarium, and the chapel makes an excellent bar.

You must certainly book well ahead in summer for this hotel. It is a popular holiday spot.

An idyllic spot beside the sea.

Food & Drink

This is a wonderful area for fresh fish and shellfish, and chief chef Nicholas Morris is a keen sauce chef, so the combination is irresistible. You may get dressed crab or Newlyn crab salad or lovely white fish such as turbot, plaice or skate as choices on the ordinary menu, which is excellent value. But if you want crab or lobster Thermidor or Newberg, or a large fresh Dover sole or crayfish tails in whisky, tomato and cheese sauce, you must pay a little more and choose from the card. That is not dear by most good hotel standards., You can get locally smoked trout, mackerel or salmon, too. And what I am told is gorgeous Bouillabaisse made of local fish, cooked to order. I don't care much for Bouillabaisse. I would take his Lobster Bisque.

There are five choices of starters and of main dishes on the menu. Nicholas Morris realizes that however well you make a sauce, there are always some Britons (and Americans) who want none of your sauces and will stick to 'good plain cooking'. He will pander to them. He offers Tournedos Rossini, for instance – fillet steak pan fried in butter in Madeira sauce topped with pâté and truffle. 'May be served plain', the menu tells us. The menu is in English, the card in French, with English descriptions. A quaint old gastronomic snobbery!

The house wines are three from Germany – dry, medium and rosé, a French dry white blend, and a fruity smooth

Minervois red from near Carcassonne in Southern France which many enthusiastic drinkers believe should have an Appellation Controlée rating.

It has improved enormously in twenty years through better tending and vinification since the days when it was drowned in imported Algerian. That is what EEC competition from good cheap Italian wines has done for some wines of Provence and Auvergne. This is particularly true of Corbières, of which there is also a good example cheap on this list – good body, dry, fruity; bad ones are still like battery acid.

There are several interesting wines here. From Germany, a luscious Mittelheimer Beerenauslese, which means made from late gathered grapes individually chosen from each bunch, and, even rarer, an Auslese Eiswein, with grapes allowed to stay on the vine until iced-up with frost, picked early in the morning while the frost is still on them. It is said to be much better than an ordinary Auslese wine, but I have not had enough to know.

A 1968 Château Latour claret is cheap by market prices. Latour is my very favourite. There is also a full blooded, full bodied, strong Bull's Blood of Eger from Hungary at a fifth of the price, and that would go well with the Tournedos Rossini. Cheaper still is a full-bodied Othello red from Cyprus. Not for me, thank you. I can still work up a hangover by just recalling a Cyprus wine festival.

There is so much of interest to see in this part of Cornwall that I suggest going to the Tourist Information Centre, Alverton Street, Penzance – (0736) 2207 – to pick up pamphlets called 'Discover the Land's End Peninsula' and 'Where to go in Penwith'.

The north coast of the peninsula is thrashed by Atlantic rollers, the south more protected. Sennen Cove, just north of Land's End, is the major surfing centre of Britain. Land's End itself, privately owned and very commercialized, is something of a disappointment unless you dream of King Arthur's Lost Land of Lyonesse, said to have joined the Scilly Isles to the mainland until swamped by the sea. The peninsula is a lovely area with wide sandy bays, including Penzance, Sennen, St Ives and

Porthleven, towering cliffs covered with heather and gorse, photogenic fishing villages clinging to rock, subtropical gardens. Penzance is a lively, charming resort with a huge beach and harbour used by fishing boats and the Scillonian ferry to the Isles of Scilly (also reached by helicopter from the local airfield). The Meteorological Office says that over the year the Scillies and Penzance areas are the warmest places in Britain, which is why they are known for daffodils and other narcissi often reaching London before Christmas, and for early vegetables. Scilly Rock is also a graveyard for ships. Diver Roland Morris and his team brought up some wonderful treasures in the 1960s from the Naval flagship Association, wrecked in 1707 with 2,000 dead. You can see many in Penzance Guildhall and in Morris's 'Admiral

Benbow' pub-restaurant, an old smuggling inn in Chapel Street.

Newlyn, two miles S of Penzance, is an important fishing port. Also an art centre with the Passmore Edwards gallery.

St Michael's Mount, an isle off Penzance in Mount's Bay, is reached by a causeway at low tide, otherwise in small boats. The castle, originally a Benedictine monastery, has been home for the St Aubyn family for generations and is now owned by the National Trust. Mousehole (2m S of Newlyn) is a quaint old fishing village, favourite of artists; it was burned by the Spaniards in 1595.

Among dozens of interesting places are Minack Theatre at Porthcurno (6m W of Lamorna), open air theatre built in her garden on the cliff edge by a girl in 1932. It now has summer season with good

visiting companies. A real
storm came up once during a
performance of The Tempest
and a shipwrecked sailor
climbed the cliff and appeared
on stage! Geevor is one of the
last tin and copper mines,
with museum (near St Just).

St Ives (on north coast) is a
lovely old former fishing town
with cobbled streets and old
cottages, now a resort crowded
in summer. It has always had
an artists' colony since
Whistler and Sickert
discovered it. Sculptress

Barbara Hepworth and painter
Ben Nicholson opened a
gallery in 1949. Now there is a
Hepworth Museum.
  See also Meudon Hotel,
Mawnan Smith, page 98, and
Penmere Manor, Falmouth,
page 118.

LINDEN HALL

**Linden Hall Hotel
Longhorsley, Morpeth,
Northumberland (leave A1
just N of Morpeth, take A697).
Telephone: (0670) 56611.
DBB C–D;
SBB C;
very good weekend dinner,
BB terms.
Open all year.
Dinner and lunch card C–D.
Credit cards: Euro, Visa,
Amex, Diners.**

A magnificent hotel, undoubtedly one of the most beautiful in Europe, and cheaper than I expected. It was converted in 1978 from a Georgian country mansion with a fine Tuscan portico in 399 acres of beautifully-kept park and woodland and with a mile-long drive. Its sweeping staircase,• domed inner hall and the perfect proportions of its rooms and windows have made it a Grade II building of architectural importance. Its antique furnishings, fine fabrics and nearly faultless decor make it a joy to wander around. Even the cocktail bar has a white marble Adam fireplace.

It is all elegant and beautiful but not a stuffy museum. And it also has such modern additions as a sauna, solarium, as well as hard tennis court, billiard room, games and table tennis room and woodland adventure play area for children.

The dining room, in beautiful blue, is a delight. Each bedroom is very individually furnished and decorated with thoughtful extras, including local mineral water from an underground spring. Some are on the ground floor around a pleasant cobbled garden, which is helpful if you are disabled. It seemed almost criminal last time to be alone in the enormous four-poster bed in my huge, luxurious pink room. It was certainly bad organization. A criticism – the Victorian conservatory deserves vines, not cacti!

If you feel like the simple life, there is a beamed pub serving bar snacks in an old coach house in the grounds.

The house was designed in 1812 by Charles Monck and the celebrated John Dobson for a banker Sheriff of Northumberland and Liberal Party leader. Now it is owned by a Newcastle travel agency. The director, Alan Blenkinsop, is as fine a host as almost any owner I have met and has helped to revive local village life, too, including restarting the village cricket team on a pitch inside the hotel park, to the wonderment of American guests.

Food&Drink

My advice is to try anything smoked – salmon, kipper, duck, chicken, ham, kipper or haddock for breakfast. It will almost certainly have been smoked over oak by Mr Robson of Craster on the nearby coast, and he is the master. I have always regarded Scottish smoked salmon from Speyside or Bute as the best in the world. But this Craster Northumber-land salmon is as good as any – tender, succulent, fairly heavily smoked but keeping the subtle salmon flavour.

It is a glorious starter, with only a touch of lemon juice, or in a mousse layered with sole

and served with mint and yoghurt sauce. A superb main course is local salmon poached in white wine and peppercorns, garnished with Craster smoked salmon and a little tart filled with caviar. There is even smoked salmon soup.

John Blackmore cooks some interesting dishes, without the excesses of invention fashionable among many chefs today. He gets some lovely fish from the coast as well as good salmon and trout, and cooks it well. An unusual combination that works is halibut wrapped in thin Parma ham slices and spinach leaf, poached in white wine and served with hollandaise sauce. And he has an unusual sauce made with smoked salmon and baked nuts which enhances the taste of scallops considerably.

After smoked salmon I chose for my last dinner noisette of lamb stuffed with duck pâté, covered in puff pastry, served on onion purée with a Madeira sauce and truffle. It was full of flavour, tender and juicy. But if you fancy simpler cooking than the dishes on the menu, you simply ask the restaurant manager. The same with vegetables – lightly cooked, unless you ask for them to be cooked longer. There is a choice of four vegetables – all fresh, many from the hotel's garden, and two sorts of potato. Portions are large here – no one dare serve slivers of vegetables and miniscule meat portions in the North of England.

Cheeses include a soft natural sheep's cheese from Mark Robertson's Redesdale Sheep Dairy near Otterburn and five more of his organic sheep cheeses. His yoghurt is available at breakfast, too. Breakfast is quite an occasion here, with Craster kippers and grilled lemon sole among many choices. Freshly baked bread and croissant, too.

David Hair, the Wine Butler, was Prestige Sommelier of the

year in 1985 and the list is certainly worthy of such a magnificent hotel. At my last dinner I was so carried away by the beautiful dining room and perfect table setting that I chose a 1970 Château Talbot claret. Gorgeous! General Talbot, the great old soldier, may have lost finally to Joan of Arc but the wine from his château is still a winner.

There is something for every taste and every pocket from £6.50 a bottle upwards, including wines from Lebanon, Australia, and England. For a white wine, you could take the chance to try Rhône whites, fairly rare in Britain – Crozes Hermitage, Hermitage Blanc and a good Châteauneuf-du-Pape – (Château de Beaucastel).

The hotel supplies pamphlets of interesting drives of 75–100 miles around Northumberland and Durham, including a tour of the coast up to the river Tweed at Berwick (see Greywalls, Gullane, page 55, and Breamish House Hotel, Powburn, page 24), the Northumbria National Park, to the Scottish Border at Coldstream and huge modern border forest of Kielder, taking in the wild white cattle herd at Chillingham (see Breamish House Hotel); Durham, its cathedral, with 900-year-old

treasures, and Washington Old Hall, ancestral home of George Washington's family; and Hadrian's Roman Wall, built to discourage the Scots from moving south. The Kielder forest and reservoir offer good sailing, superb fishing and beautiful walks.

South of Alnwick (Percy Castle, see Breamish House Hotel, page 24) is Warkworth, where the river Coquet reaches the sea – one of the best salmon and trout rivers in the north. There is a rare mediaeval bridge with a tower

and the ruins of a castle mentioned by Shakespeare in Henry IV ('worm-eaten hold of regged stone'). It was the birthplace of Hotspur (Sir Henry Percy) killed in 1403 fighting Henry IV at Shrewsbury. Eider ducks breed on Coquet Isle.

Newcastle is twenty miles SE of Longhorsley.

Rothbury (8m NW through Coquet Dale) is a nice village on a steep bank by the river; excellent fishing. It was already there when the Normans invaded in 1066.

I rate it with the best French "Relais et Châteaux" hotels.

Lords of the Manor Hotel

Lords of the Manor Hotel
Upper Slaughter,
nr Bourton-on-the-Water,
Cheltenham, Gloucestershire
GL54 2JD (just off A429
signposted going N after
Bourton-on-the-Water).
Telephone: Cotswold (0451)
20243.
DBB C–D;
SBB B.
Dinner card B–C;
lunch A.
Closed January 6–19.
Credit cards: Euro, Visa,
Amex, Diners.

Follow the Fosse Way (A429) north-east from Cirencester, as the Romans did, and striding the pretty Windrush river is Bourton-on-the-Water, one of Britain's loveliest villages and most crowded with tourists. But half a mile on, across the Way, a lane is signposted 'The Slaughters'. Immediately you are lost in a silent, leafy world of narrow lanes, hills and old houses in honey Cotswold stone. Upper Slaughter, on the trout-rich river Eye, is a true haven of peace, with no new building since 1904 and no through traffic. The beautiful long stone house set among lawns and flowers below a hill planted with summer wheat is the former Rectory, home of the Witts family for 200 years. They were Rectors for four generations (1763–1913) and have been Lords of the Manor since 1852. The present head of the family converted their home into an hotel in 1972, and I do not know any hotel more tranquil yet alive and lived-in. I hope to go back many times.

The house was built in the seventeenth century, with additions in the eighteenth and nineteenth centuries, which is why bedrooms vary in size. All are comfortably and interestingly furnished with antiques and period pieces, and with good carpeted bathrooms. A garden room with wicker furniture and an elegant and very comfortable lounge have big windows with views of the grounds, so has the excellent bar. Here you meet local people as well as passing travellers. The dining room, open plan, is made from three smaller rooms, making it coy and intimate, with old, rich wood tables and chairs.

There is a lake in the grounds. The river runs through and guests have free brown trout fishing in season (March-October) but you must return the fish to the water.

This lovely Cotswold hideout is for holding hands, relaxing and pondering.

Sherry on the Rectory lawn before dinner.

Food & Drink

The dishes served in the attractive dining rooms have become more sophisticated and interesting under chef Vincent Tobin than before. They change daily, but he usually serves a roast joint as one choice. His own specialities are mousse of wild Avon perch in lemon mousseline sauce and salad of quail cooked in the hotel smoker over oak wood, served with a dressing of honey and mustard. For a main course he likes to serve a compote of local wild wood pigeon marinated in white Bordeaux, served with smoked bacon, field mush-rooms and Crème de Cassis, or roast best-end of veal stuffed with pork and tarragon, with a shallot and white vinegar butter sauce. His special sweets are dark chocolate curd cake and poached pears in crème de menthe syrup. Eat a meal made up of these and you should be very happy, even if not slimmer.

He smokes over oak many meats and fishes for starters, including wild salmon, local trout, turkey and wild duck, and also chicken, served with crisp fresh vegetables and a light horseradish sauce.

His special dishes of the day are extra interesting. Recently I was offered sautéed medal-lions of wild Welsh boar, marinated in Grand Marnier, served with a Seville orange sauce. Absolutely delicious. He grills Scotch beef pretty well, too, or serves it with something like melted Brie cheese and a sauce of port wine and beef marrow.

His soups are excellent, including clam chowder, leek and parsnip with toasted almonds, thick vegetable with Jersey cream. The walled garden supplies many of the fine vegetables.

I think that Vincent Tobin, when he has been here a little longer, will be getting accolades from many guides.

The hotel has pleasant red and white house wine, specially bottled, labelled with a copy of a nineteenth-century watercolour of the hotel as The Rectory, and reasonably priced; but the white is too medium for me, even as an aperitif. A little dearer is a very nice red Côtes de Ventoux, light, fresh, and rather pale red, one of the latest wines to be given an official appellation and pleasant drunk with poultry. These red wines around the Mont Ventoux area in the Vaucluse are underestimated in Britain.

The Mouton Cadet is cheap,

the good Cheval Noir Grand Cru St Emilion 1978 is very good value, so is the 1976 Château Livran Médoc, a wine always worth seeking to drink with anything from pâté through meats and poultry to cheese.

There is a fairly rare white Burgundy on the list, St Aubin, which would go well with that wild Avon perch or the smoked fish.

The fine wines at £20 upwards, both claret and Bur-

gundy, are beautifully chosen and make me very envious, especially the 1976 Burgundies from the négociant Louis Latour. His Chambolle Musigny of 1976 is one of the classiest wines of Burgundy still around. Les Epenots from Domaine de Courcel is probably the best of Pommard wines — sturdy with finesse. Louis Latour should know. His great great grandfather was planting vines successfully around those parts.

 Go to Bourton-on-the-Water early morning, at sunset or outside the tourist season. It is such a lovely spot, with the little river running beside the main street.

Upper Slaughter's Norman church has the tomb of the Rev. F. E. Witts, Victorian author of The Diary of a Cotswold Parson. *At Eyeford (½m) Milton is said to have written much of* Paradise Lost. *Next to the hotel is an Elizabethan manor house built by the Slaughter family who emigrated to America in the eighteenth century (open Friday p.m. in summer).*

Lower Slaughter (1m) has another beautiful manor and other fine houses. Lower and Upper Swell, on river Dikler (2m), are very attractive; Roman jewels and coins were found when Lower Swell church was being restored.

Cheltenham (17m W A429, A436), a spa whose healthy waters were discovered in 1715 when someone studied

the habits of healthy pigeons and found a mineral spring. Pump room opened 1738. Waters were used to treat liver complaints of army officers and colonial administrators returning from the tropics. A new town was laid out — wide streets of Georgian houses with tree-shaded open spaces which survive, though now jet aircraft are designed and assembled in Cheltenham. Annual music festival ranges from concerts of British composers to jazz, folk and a Bach choir. Racecourse where Cheltenham Gold Cup is run. Do see the Georgian Promenade and Montpelier

Walk Georgian shopping precinct.

For Blenheim Palace, home of the Churchills (including the great soldier the Duke of Marlborough), see the Feathers, Woodstock, page 49.

For Broadway area, see Lygon Arms, Broadway, page 91.

For Cotswold Farm Park with its rare farm animals, including Soay sheep unchanged since domestication by Stone Age man and prehistoric pigs with striped piglets, pick up B4068 (1m N of Upper Slaughter), turn left, then right (signposted).

The Lygon Arms
Broadway, Worcestershire
WR12 7DU (on A44 6m SE of
Evesham and on A46
Cheltenham–Stratford-on-
Avon).
Telephone: Broadway (0386)
852255.
DBB F;
SBB C.
Dinner C;
lunch A.
Open all year.
Credit cards: Euro, Visa,
Amex, Diners.

The rebirth of the great British innkeeping tradition began in 1945 in this lovely old Cotswold coaching inn which has served travellers well for 450 years in this truly beautiful village. I saw it happen. Built in 1520, the Lygon (originally the White Hart) had been bought in 1904 by the Russell family. They started a workshop to restore antiques and make new pieces for the inn, ended by designing and hand-making superb furniture exported to Middle East palaces, embassies in Moscow and millionaires' mansions in California.

Like most hotels, it ran down in the war through lack of labour and rationing of everything from bread to bed linen.

In 1945 Gordon Russell, world-famous designer, appointed as manager a young Australian back from the war – Douglas Barrington. He was a perfectionist. Within a year the hotel had an international reputation for service and imaginative meals (despite continued rationing).

Forty years later the Lygon is known world wide for excel-

lence – a member of the British Prestige Hotels, of France's Relais et Châteaux hotels, and of the Swiss-inspired Leading Hotels of the World. And Douglas Barrington, the owner, is doyen of British hotel-keepers.

Old adjoining properties have been taken over, like the eighteenth-century Great Hall with a minstrels' gallery and heraldic frieze – long ago a village meeting place, now the Lygon's restaurant. A new wing has been built next to the lovely quiet garden. But the Lygon is little changed, with its higgledy-piggledy maze of rooms, large and small, which give it a cosy feeling, its magnificent antiques, from priceless china to Elizabethan tables and a fourposter bed carved '1620', the year the *Mayflower* sailed, and its room where Oliver Cromwell slept the night before he beat Charles I (another former guest) at the battle of Worcester. The bedrooms necessarily vary in size, but all the old ones have wonderful antique furniture, the new ones beautiful tradi-

tional furniture. Also books, flowers, a welcoming glass of sherry and fine bathrooms. My last room, besides huge old oak beams, centuries-old heavy door and mullioned windows, had an efficient electrical trouser press and flask of iced water. Not exactly 1520 style. They wore pantaloons then.

The service is so smooth and friendly that an American girl told me that she felt almost embarrassed at so much attention. Not me. I only get upset at being 'processed', as modern hotels call serving you.

The greatest of English Inns.

Food & Drink

The new chef, Alain Dubois, came from Hunstrete Manor, another pricey hotel, and aims to provide traditional English cooking with a light touch combined with classical French cooking. This does not seem to have impressed some guides but has brought many satisfied customers, especially Americans and people who drive a long way just to dine here. So would I.

On the ordinary dinner menu last time I was offered a choice of chicken terrine with Roquefort, succulent fresh asparagus with salad or game soup with port, really gamey and delicious. The main course was leg of spring lamb with fresh mint, rump steak with peppercorns, brandy and cream, or a panache of seafood with lobster sauce, which I found delicious, as it included beautifully fresh Hebridean oysters and truly soft and flavoursome young scallops. The vegetables were perfectly cooked and included crisp young French beans and mange-touts and delicious young, firm courgettes, and we had new and real Dauphinoise potatoes. I like vegetables very lightly cooked but you may have them cooked longer. For dessert, from a magnificent choice, I took a light, mouth-filling, creamy gâteau with fresh young strawberries and Cointreau.

This may sound a rather ordinary meal, but the cooking was far above ordinary. He roasts meat to perfection. Try roast best end of lamb, coated with herb breadcrumbs and garlic. He is known, too, for cooking game – try venison with wild mushrooms in marc de Bourgogne, and for fish. His crayfish soufflé sent a gastronome friend into near raptures and another was raving about his fairly simple dish of suprême of turbot with crayfish mousseline and lobster sauce.

On the card is a little note: 'If you would prefer your dishes served in a plain manner or grilled, we would be happy to provide this.' I know that one or two Americans have taken him up on this. I wonder if any Frenchman will?

The hotel has a Goblet's Wine Bar where you can get some very good one- to three-course lunches, cooked in the hotel kitchen – with good choice of wine.

There is a superbly-chosen list of wines in the restaurant. The great Mistress of Wine Serena Sutcliffe says in the introduction: 'I would particularly point out the fine German Riesling wines, when so many brews from this country are rather anonymous sugary liquids.' How right!

There are wines for every taste, occasion, from a light lunch to a celebration dinner, and for most pockets, with prices between £6 and £80 a bottle.

For the roasts, I suggest in the lower price range fruity young Julienas 1983 Les Envaux, an under-rated Loire Champigny from Saumur, or a wine which would also go very well with my game soup or the venison, a Garrafeira from northern Portugal's Dao river area. Dao wine is strong, deep red and full of body, earthy and irony at first, becoming velvety, like this one, when five or six years old. It keeps well. In the medium price range, I would go for the 1977 Château Talbot, generous and fruity, probably because it matures in huge oak vats; one of my favourite wines, and much cheaper here than in most places. If you prefer Burgundy, try the 1979 Gevrey-Chambertin, one of the chosen wines of the Chevaliers du Tastevin in their pleasant annual duty.

For celebration wines (with rich uncle George paying) there is a heart-tearing choice between Haut Brion 1967, Cheval Blanc 1967 from St Emilion, a 1976 Lafite-Rothschild, or a delectable Burgundy, a velvety 1976 Richebourg from the Domaine of Charles Noeffat. If you have never tasted Richebourg (and it is not always around), grab any chance you get.

Before tourism was accepted in Britain, Broadway was called scathingly 'The Painted Lady of the Cotswolds'. Now the Lygon Arms holds the Queen's Award for its hospitality to foreign visitors!

The main street of Broadway is crowded with daytime tourists in high season, and its shops are mostly aimed at them. But Lygon guests seem to enjoy window shopping. And it clears in the evening. The Cotswold country is one of Britain's beautiful gems, with much of its beauty in the stone buildings and villages. The hotel has prepared a pamphlet of walks and car tours. The first takes you round local villages, including Chipping Campden, the Slaughters (see Lords of the Manor Hotel, page 91), Burford, Winchcombe (Sudeley Castle, home of Katherine Parr, Henry VIII's final wife; ruined, reconstructed in 1858 by Sir Gilbert Scott).

Others go to Cirencester (see Burleigh Court Hotel, Minchinhampton, page 27); to

Stratford-on-Avon (see
Billesley Manor Hotel,
page 14) and Warwick
(see Regent Hotel, Leamington
Spa, page 134); Ross-on-Wye
(see Pengethley Hotel,
Ross-on-Wye, page 114),
Wye Valley, Severn Bridge,
Gloucester, Cheltenham

(see Burleigh Court Hotel,
Minchinhampton, page 27);
and Blenheim Palace, Bladon
(grave of Sir Winston
Churchill) and Oxford (see
Feathers, Woodstock, page 49,
and Weston Manor, Weston-
on-the-Green, page 154).
  Snowshill (2½m from

Broadway) is a Tudor
mansion containing
collections of musical
instruments, clocks, toys and
bicycles (opening times –
Wednesday to Sunday May–
September; Saturday–Sunday
April–October; 11a.m.–1p.m.;
2–5p.m.) National Trust.

**Maes-y-Neuadd Hotel
Talsarnau, near Harlech,
Gwynedd, North Wales
LL47 6YA (2m SE of Talsarnau
on unclassified road off
B4573).
Telephone: Harlech (0766)
780200.
BB per person with dinner A.
Dinner B.
Closed January.
Credit cards: Euro, Visa,
Amex, Diners.**

I cannot pronounce the name of this welcoming hotel, either! It is something like 'Mice-er-Nayath' and means the Hall in the Fields. By any name, it is a lovely old Welsh granite and slate house on a mountainside with superb views across Snowdonia National Park. The oldest part is fourteenth century, and contains a cosy bar with an inglenook, and two beamed bedrooms above it. The bedrooms in the sixteenth-century additions have beams, too, and large, light bedrooms in the eighteenth-century addition have views to Snowdon mountain.

Beyond the seven-and-a-half acre grounds of lawns, orchard and paddock is simply magnificent countryside for walking, riding, climbing and exploring by car. The sea is only three miles away, and so is Royal St David's Golf Course, scene of amateur championships.

The hotel is run by two families, the Slatters and the Horsfalls, and between them they provide good service with a very relaxed atmosphere and good family cooking of local food. It is a place to relax, to get fit or both. You will find yourself leaving the car behind most days and just wandering.

Food & Drink

Local trout, sea trout, salmon and crab, with succulent Welsh lamb cooked in several ways, are the basis of menus which change with seasons and availability of local produce. Olive Horsfall, June Slatter and Andrew Price share the cooking and produce between them a good variety of dishes, including Gregyn Gleison Stiw, which is mussels stewed with garlic and herbs and Pwdin Mynwy, which every good Welsh speaker knows is what the English call Monmouth pudding, topped with meringue.

The crab starters are delightful, both crab pancakes, rolled in breadcrumbs and fried, and crab éclairs of deliciously light choux pastry filled with a light crab mixture. A smooth terrine of prawns and smoked salmon is served in pancakes. Tomatoes are stuffed with a soufflé-style gruyère cheese filling and baked.

Breast of duck is fried in slices and served with sauce made from the pan juices, white wine and green peppers. It is not, as with Nouvelle Cuisine, served with shavings of carrot and kiwi fruit but with good-sized portions of three very fresh vegetables. But kiwi fruit is served with strawberries and cream in puff pastry. A main dish is provided for vegetarians. When it is Stilton and vegetable pie, some non-believers order it, too.

Dinner is excellent value. So are the wines, of which there is a very good choice for a small country hotel such as this.

They range from a really cheap vin de table bottled in Burgundy to a Mouton-Rothschild 1971. Among whites, the cheap Entre-Deux-Mers is outstanding value and so is La Ferronière Muscadet. In reds I recommend the fruity Château du Breuil Bordeaux Cissac. The

Fleurie La Madonne is good value. Les Suchots Vosne Romanée, a heady, delightful wine with a lovely bouquet, is one of the best commune wines of this area of Burgundy which can produce some of the finest wines in the world.

If you are prepared to lash out a bit on wine, watch the list of Bin Ends, which can include some real winners, like a 1976 Domaine du Château de Puligny-Montrachet which we spotted there recently. What a lovely wine to accompany those crab dishes or the lamb if you prefer white to red.

LOCAL DRIVES *This is some of the loveliest countryside in Britain, and the beaches are excellent, too. A mile west of Talsarnau you reach the huge broad sandy estuary where the Glaslyn and Dwyryd rivers meet. Part is the Morfa Harlech nature reserve, with colonies of wading birds. The sands stretch almost all the way along Tremadog Bay to Shell Island (for Harlech, 4m from the hotel, and Shell Island, see Palé Hall Hotel, page 111). Eastwards on Lake Bala (see Palé Hall Hotel) is the sleepy old town of Bala which was a famous centre of Methodism. People from here emigrated to Patagonia in South America in 1865. Their descendants still speak Welsh as well as Spanish. The road from Bala to Dinas Mawddwy southward is magnificent (but narrow) and Bwlch y Groes (Pass of the Cross) is at 1790ft the highest road in Wales.*

Portmeirion, the Italian-style village on the edge of the Lleyn Peninsula, is five miles round the estuary from Talsarnau. For information on this show village and the whole lovely Lleyn Peninsula, see Porth Tocyn Hotel, Abersoch, page 124.

The hotel owners will tell you where to find excellent trout fishing, as well as sailing, boating and horse riding.

Meudon Hotel
Mawnan Smith, Falmouth,
Cornwall TR11 5HT.
Telephone: (0326) 250541.
DBB D;
SBB B.
Dinner B (5 courses);
lunch A.
Closed mid-November to mid-
February.
Credit cards: Euro, Visa,
Amex, Diners.

The garden is so magnificent that it is designated an area of 'Outstanding Natural Beauty', with the surrounding 200 acres of National Trust-owned coastline between the rivers Fal and Helford. Covering eight and a half acres, it was laid out by Capability Brown in the eighteenth century and is semi-tropical, with mimosa, camellias, azaleas, eucalyptus and superb rhododendrons, and leads to a private beach by the sea. It has been restored by Harry Pilgrim and his wife since they turned the house into an hotel in 1964.

The house, alas, is not so beautiful, mainly because of an odd stubby castellated tower. Originally, 300 years ago, it was two coastguard cottages on this coast then known for smuggling, wrecking and the odd bit of piracy. It is comfortable inside, with good garden views, and the bedrooms are in a handsome modern block, joined to the main building by a lounge. Many have fine garden views. They have good fitted furniture and neat bathrooms. The main lounge is large, the bar comfortable and elegant.

It is a friendly, sympathetic hotel, a fine centre for quiet walks, and for fishermen, sailors and gardening enthusiasts. Sea angling includes shark and conger eels. You can fish for trout in local reservoirs and streams. From Falmouth nearby you can hire a boat to sail yourself or with a skipper. It is a good area for windsurfing, too.

Alan Webb is back as Chef. That is good news to any friends of Meudon who had not heard yet. After he left a few years ago, cooking standards definitely fell. All is back to the standards that rightly won Meudon accolades. You can now again enjoy the meal as much as the garden flowers as you sit in the fine glass-covered terrace dining room.

He cooks leg of lamb in hay, as we did in the Boy Scouts, but much better. He serves fine local meat, shellfish and fish,

mostly with his own special sauces, and good fresh local vegetables. If you ask, he will give you oysters fresh from the Helford river, crab or lobster fresh landed at Falmouth and superbly cooked. Do try his crab Thermidor. Delicious. You pay a supplement, of course, for such delicacies, though I had a crab starter on the ordinary menu last time.

Alan's specialities include some lovely dishes – tomato and orange soup, Mexican fish chowder, scampi in Pernod sauce, grilled beef in green pepper and sour cream sauce. I like his carrots cooked in juice of fresh oranges.

Among interesting sweets is one from Franche-Comté, strawberry Malakoff (in almond pastry).

Harry Pilgrim gives you under the heading 'Director's Selection' his own choice of light wines, including a choice of 1976 or 1979 Giscour Margaux. I could imagine an Englishman picking the 1976 (an unusually rich and full wine from this important third growth property) and most Frenchmen picking the 1979 because that was an exceptional year for Margaux and because the French seem to drink Bordeaux wines fairly young – often too young. That is why so many prefer Burgundy, which matures more quickly.

The rest of the list is down-to-earth, with reliable wines and attractive prices. Very reasonable choice, too. If you catch a shark, it will not cost you a fortune to celebrate while Alan is frying it for you!

Start with a dozen oysters – courtesy of Prince Charles!

For Falmouth (6m N), Pendennis Castle, St Mawes, Truro, Trelissick Gardens, see Penmere Manor, Falmouth page 118.

The Helford Passage joining the sea to the Helford river is a mile away. Here are Glendurgan Gardens, in a valley, with fine trees and shrubs, and a maze (open March–October Monday, Wednesday, Friday). In a secretive creek called Porth Navas is a sailing club and nearby the great oyster beds owned by Prince Charles as Duke of Cornwall. You can watch them being hauled from the sea, then eat them. Further up river is a tiny tidal port, Gweek, with a sanctuary for seals washed up around the Cornish coast. Feeding times are usually 11a.m. and 4.30p.m. Four miles S of Gweek on B3293 is Goonhilly Downs, the important satellite communication station where history was made in 1962 with first space satellite picture transmission with the US. The old village of Helford (across Helford river by pedestrian ferry from Helford Passage) is an exquisite village with rows of white houses, thatched or grey slated, each side of a narrow creek with swans and boats, all among flowers and trees. Half a mile W is Frenchman's Creek, made famous by Daphne du Maurier's novel. It is best seen by boat. At Mawgan nearby is a Jacobean mansion, Trelowarren, with a chapel and exhibitions changing periodically (pictures, musical instruments, etc.)

open March–Christmas, Tuesdays–Sundays; also Cornish Craft Association exhibits.

Helston's ancient Furry Dance is on May 8. At 7a.m. the band starts to play and from then until pub closing time there is dancing up and down the hilly streets and in and out of houses and shops. Most of the people take part, some in top hats and costume. It is a pre-Christian survival. It seems that the devil dropped a rock on the town and the people danced with joy because it did little damage. In the old Butter Market is a museum with a fine old cider mill, a grist mill, and old implements. In Coinagehall Street is the cottage of Bob Fitzsimmons, boxer who in 1897 won the world heavyweight championship by knocking out 'Gentleman Jim' Corbett of the US. Cornwall's Aero Park and

Flambard's Village at Helston is life-size re-creation of Victorian village, also of a wartime street in the Blitz. Superb historic aeroplanes, helicopters, vehicles. (Open Easter–October.)

N three miles from Helston is Poldark Mine, Wendron – underground tin mine workings with waterwheel chamber, now a museum; also gardens and battery powered racing cars for children. Six miles S at Poldhu Point is where Marconi's assistant broadcast the first Transatlantic radio message to Marconi in St John's, Newfoundland. News of the Titanic disaster was first heard here. The Looe (2m SW), near fishing port of Porthleven, is one of the many lakes where King Arthur's sword Excalibur was cast . . .

For Penzance, St Ives and Land's End, see Lamorna Cove Hotel, Lamorna, page 80.

Middlethorpe Hall
Bishopthorpe Road, York
YO2 1QP (on edge of York
racecourse, marked turning
off A1036 Tadcaster road,
turning marked
Bishopthorpe; ½m past
village down Bishopthorpe
road).
Telephone: York (0904)
641241.
DBB D;
suites DBB F;
BBB C.
Dinner C;
lunch A (including ½ bottle of
wine).
Open all year.
Credit cards: Euro, Visa,
Amex, Diners.

York is one of the finest cities in the world. Roman, medi-aeval, rich in historic treasures, yet an active, lively modern city, not a museum piece. It has always had good cosy little hotels and latterly some efficient modern business hotels, but lacked really good hotels of character where you are a name, not a room number in a computer.

Middlethorpe has filled the gap excellently, and although only one and a half miles from the station and the cathedral, is in a tranquil spot away from traffic and tourists – except on race days. York racecourse is so near that you could get a sneak view of the 3.30.

A truly elegant house of 1699 in Queen Anne style of red Flemish bond brick, it was in a bizarre state of disrepair as a night club when bought in 1980 by Historic House Hotels, second of the fine old houses they have saved from derelic-tion. They have made a magni-ficent job of it, and with its fine carved oak staircase, old panel-ling and appropriate eight-eenth-century style furniture

and pictures, it is again a stately house, even if some portraits do look like 'instant ancestors'. It is also comfortable, with a beautiful big lounge-writing room where drinks and coffee are normally served and another fine lounge upstairs, both with garden views. The two con-necting dining rooms give a more intimate touch than one big one. Table settings are immaculate, the young staff friendly and helpful. A York-shireman, the young manager Malcolm Broadbent has a lot of experience in France and London. He came from the Stafford. He is rightly proud of Middlethorpe, a happy, friendly hotel deserving its AA Three Red Stars.

I had a big but intimately comfortable bedroom with a heated trouser press which really worked and a pretty Edwardian style bathroom with flowers and nicknacks. There were nicknacks every-where, in keeping with the period. I was a little afraid of breaking one!

Middlethorpe was a girls' school not so long ago. It

seemed a shame to waste my vast comfortable bed on myself. I wondered what would happen if I rang for the companionship of a mistress. Some bedrooms are in the eighteenth-century stable-block.

Not the easiest part of saving Middlethorpe Hall was restoring thirty acres of grounds. The garden and park look as if they were never overgrown. Hundreds of trees planted, the ruined seventeenth-century dovecote restored, the lake reformed, and a ha-ha constructed (a sunken fence, not taped laughter for an American chat-show).

Food & Drink

Aiden McCormack is not only a good chef – he is versatile. Four years ago he was at Chewton Glen as No 2 to the great French chef Christian Delteil. He was cooking dishes which, if not Nouvelle Cuisine, were modern, unusual and creative. Now he has proved that he can satisfy Yorkshire tastes and appetites, with traditional British cooking which is tasty and satisfying without lying heavy on the diner. Some would say that this is the more difficult trick. Chewton Glen diners are mostly enthusiasts, anxious to try new eating experiences. In Yorkshire they are big eaters who know what they want and expect it to be provided in some quantity. I know. I used to live outside York in villages. I love the place, too.

Aiden allows himself a few flourishes – like an excellent fresh ravioli filled with salmon and fennel in a cream herb sauce as a starter, a ginger and tomato sauce with scallops, and sometimes the inevitable Nouvelle flag-carrier – half-raw duck breasts in raspberry vinegar sauce. But more often he is judged by the quality and cooking of his roasts, fillets and chops, and breasts of pheasant. They are very good. His vegetables are excellent. Many come from the kitchen garden, recently restored. I had superb mange-tout peas and baby carrots, lightly cooked. If you prefer them cooked longer, just ask. Ask early, too, for the delicious Drambuie soufflé.

You can have Welsh Rarebit instead of a sweet. Good! My little favourite has been banished from most hotel menus, along with all such savouries, in the name of keeping down our weight.

The wine list is well chosen for a fairly short list but a little pricey, with few surprises. I noticed one or two cheaper wines on the banqueting list for the separate dining room for functions which might well have appeared on the ordinary list; like a white Rully and a Croze Hermitage.

I was delighted to find a red Bouzy, the still wine of the Champagne. It is rare outside the Champagne area, therefore not desperately cheap, but much under-rated and by no means just a substitute for Burgundy, which some wine writers call it. It is a fine partner to many of Aiden's main courses – and the Welsh Rarebit.

You will never tire of York.

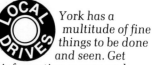

York has a multitude of fine things to be done and seen. Get information, a map and official guide from the excellent York Tourist Board, De Grey Rooms, Exhibition Square (tel. York 21756). The plaques on historic buildings are most helpful. Do walk round the city walls. There is 2,000 years of history inside them, and one of the most interesting sites is the new Jorvik Viking Centre showing the life of the city before the Norman Conquest in 1066. The Romans set up their headquarters for subduing the wild North in 71AD. Despite recent fire damage, the Minster (cathedral) is still one of the greatest and most impressive churches on earth and the biggest mediaeval church, dwarfing most other churches, in the world. Started in 1222 and finished 250 years later, it has over 100 stained glass windows covering 800 years. When foundations were dug out to repair a 20,000 ton tower they found remains of a Roman fort, Viking strongpost Norman church and thirteenth-century cathedral foundations. So they did not fill in the undercroft.

Castle Museum's Victorian cobbled streets with buildings including condemned cell where highwayman Dick Turpin was held until hanged are interesting. Fascinating for me is the National Railway museum, including the world's fastest steam engine, the Mallard, the Advanced Passenger Train, and the Royal coaches.

York has so many little mediaeval churches that some now have other uses, like an art centre. The River Ouse runs through the city, then through woods and meadows to the edge of Middlethorpe's park and, a mile past, the Archbishop's Palace. Boat trips are delightful.

Harrogate (22m W) is a very handsome eighteenth-century spa and still a town of flowers. The old Royal Pump Room, where 1,000 glasses of sulphurous water were served in a morning, is now a museum and concert hall.

Harewood House (8m S of Harrogate) is one of the greatest houses in Britain. Robert Adam's best interior decorations, Adam's and Chippendale's most exquisite furniture, in a Palladian Mansion by John Carr in park and gardens by Capability Brown. All done around 1759 for Edwin Lascelles, first Earl of Harewood, from profits of West Indian plantations. Current Earl is a cousin to the Queen. Great paintings, fine silver, Sèvres china. Bird garden in grounds. Open daily April–October; Sunday only February, March and November.

Oakley Court Hotel
Windsor Road, Water Oakley,
nr Windsor, Berkshire
SL4 5UR
(on A308 road, halfway
between Windsor and
Maidenhead).
Telephone: Maidenhead
(0628) 74141.
DBB D–F;
SBB C.
Dinner D;
menu gourmand (6 courses) E.
Open all year.
No dogs.
Credit cards: Euro, Visa,
Amex, Diners.

This French-style gothic château built by an Englishman to comfort his homesick French wife is in one of the finest positions of any hotel in Europe – thirty-five acres of beautifully groomed gardens and grounds on the very banks of the River Thames. It has been impeccably restored, to the last inch of decorative plasterwork and oak panelling, and beautifully furnished. It has true four-star elegance but manages to keep an informal, almost intimate atmosphere. The new rooms in modern blocks are discreetly luxurious, but I do hope that increasing the number of bedrooms to 90 and improving conference facilities will not destroy the country house informality and make it a grand hotel. There is no sign of that happening yet.

The lounges, library and bar all have doors opening to the grounds, which can be viewed from the attractive dining room. Recently we had a massive bedroom in the mansion, with a large bay window overlooking the river and lawns with a fountain, and there were

more river views from the delightful bathroom where not only bathrobes but scales were provided – to be ignored by anyone taking Murdo Mac-Sween's menu gourmand.

The table in the billiard room is 300 years old.

If you get that sense of déja vu, think back to some old movies – Dracula, Tommy Steele's Half a Sixpence, Peter Sellers' Murder by Death, not to mention the ultimate horror – The Girls of St Trinian's School. They were all made here when the mansion was unoccupied, by film companies using Down Place next door. In the Second World War, Oakley Court was a training place for British and French agents dropped into France to help the Resistance.

It is all rather jollier these days. Even Dracula would probably settle for something not too lethal, like the 1971 La Tache Grand Cru Burgundy from Romanée-Conti Domaine said by some experts to be the 'perfect' wine. I noticed that Bull's Blood of Eger was not on the list.

Food & Drink

Murdo MacSween, Master Chef of Great Britain, one of the best in Europe, describes his cooking as 'classic, with modern French interpretation'. I translate that as mainly classic dishes with some light touches and very artistic presentation. He serves a magnificent and very expensive menu gourmand, a set-price slightly less-ambitious menu and an ambitious card with his speciality dishes. It is all mouth-watering and fulfilling and although you could quibble about certain small matters, he is undoubtedly a great chef for one so young by French culinary standards.

All his ingredients come fresh daily from a local market garden and the markets of London and Paris, where he has an agent shopping for him. He changes his set-price menus daily and gourmand menu and card every three months.

His gourmand menu is likely to go something like this: ter-rine of lobster and turbot encased in spinach with mint and honey cream; sliced warm, scallops with baby mange-touts and pink grapefruit in walnut oil; sorbet; fillets of beef, pork and veal sautéed with cèpes and wild mush-rooms and served in a light red wine sauce, with a generous selection of fresh vegetables and potatoes; a cheeseboard selection, then pears poached in red wine; coffee. That is a winter menu, of course. And what a feast!

He makes a splendid con-sommé, served with strips of vegetables and topped with a cheese soufflé, a smoked had-dock mousse with avocado set in a Pouilly-Fuissé wine jelly, a mousse of pistachio nuts stuf-fed with veal kidneys served on spinach, and salmon ragout of cubes of Scotch salmon poached in white wine, with cream and chive sauce, tomato and truffles.

There are plenty of more traditional dishes, too, includ-

ing a roast joint of the day, grilled lamb cutlets topped with Stilton mousse, strips of beef with a redcurrant jelly and cream sauce, veal escalope with prunes and a port wine sauce.

Desserts are delicious. Try a hot crêpe filled with hot straw-berries in Kirsch, vanilla ice and hot fruit purée. Or the lovely home-made ice creams.

House wines are good – Louis Lussac Côte-du-Rhône or Muscadet, for instance. But Murdo's cooking does deserve something better if possible, even if you must miss the superlative clarets with vin-tages like 1917, 1934 or even something as young as a 1945 Château Cheval Blanc, the greatest St Emilion. It is magni-ficent reading, this list, even if a dream world to me. I did spit a little when I saw a 1937 Château Latour Pauillac for £145 a bottle. To think that I

bought some cases of that wine at auction for under £2 a bottle in 1950 and fed it to my friends at dinner! I hope they appreciated it.

Frankly, I think that some of the good clarets are over-priced here. A 1976 La Lagune was £40 in 1985 — an exciting year but *too* pricey. I would have to settle for the much-cheaper 1978 Lamothe Cissac, which has body and flavour. Or perhaps the Chambolle Musigny 1982 because it is a Louis Jadot wine and I have tasted some good Chambolles from this shipper, quite subtle, yet with a touch of iron which I like in Burgundy. Mind you, the 1973 Bonnes Mares at twice the price would be superb — and still have the iron.

Barbara says that the Puligny-Montrachet Les Folatières was one of the best white Burgundies she has had for a very long time. I will not tell you the price because she was travelling alone and another man bought it for her!

The bar serves beers from around the world, even Mexico, China, Japan, Malaya and India. The Belgian are the best, and the dearest — a genuine trappist, the nectar made by monks, and a Mort Subite-Geuze — Sudden Death. Who would order Spanish beer with these around?

One of the best chefs in Britain.

Windsor (3m E) still revolves around the Royal castle, covering thirteen acres, largest inhabited castle in the world. Founded by William the Conqueror, it became a Royal residence of Henry I and includes additions made for Queen Victoria. Henry VIII built a chapel which Victoria turned into a shrine to her Consort, Prince Albert. St George's Chapel, built by Edward IV and altered by Henry VIII, is a magnificent example of Perpendicular architecture. It is the burial place of royalty, Henry VIII among them. The great Round Tower, built for Henry II, has fine views. The state apartments date from Edward III's reign. The precincts are open to the public daily. The state apartments are open when the Queen is not in residence. Queen Mary's dolls' house, the Albert Memorial Chapel and the old master drawings are open even when the Queen is there, St George's Chapel when no service is in progress, and the Round Tower. The 4,800 acre Great Park almost surrounds the castle. You can walk or drive through it (beware of deer). Charles II created the three-mile Long Walk and in the eighteenth century Queen Anne added a three-mile drive to Ascot, with the famous racecourse. The Great Park has the remarkable Savill Garden, with an incredible variety of plants and shrubs in twenty acres. The 150-acre lake Virginia Water was created in the eighteenth

century. A safari park SW is open daily. Across the river from Windsor is Eton, with a quaint old High Street and quaint old school, Eton College, founded in 1440 by Henry VI.

The nearest thing to a village left on this part of the Thames is Bray, between the hotel and Maidenhead, made famous in song for its sixteenth-century vicar who adjusted his religious beliefs to suit the monarch of the day. Here is the Temple of Nouvelle Cuisine in Britain, Waterside Inn, owned by the Roux brothers.

At Maidenhead the river flows beneath two fine bridges – Brunel's brick railway bridge and a balustraded road bridge. Upstream is Boulter's Lock, a beauty spot reminiscent of Jerome K. Jerome's Three Men in a Boat; then Cookham, facing a green, village of the painter Stanley Spencer (1891–1959) whose painting 'The Last Supper' hangs in the twelfth-century village church, with more paintings in King's Hall. His painting of Cookham Bridge is in London's Tate Gallery. Over the river is Cliveden, once owned by the Astors, a meeting place of top Tories, the so-called Cliveden Set, before the Second World War. Marlow has an elegant suspension bridge, and some unspoiled streets such as West Street, with Albion House where in 1817 the poet Shelley wrote The Revolt of Islam and his wife Mary wrote Frankenstein. Here the scenery is rural. Across the river is Quarry Wood with

25,000 acres of beeches. Upstream is Medmenham Abbey, eighteenth-century meeting place of the Hell Fire Club for black magic rites. Next comes Henley, where the first rowing regatta in the world was held in 1839. The event is now held every July. Then comes Sonning, where the river divides round islands. You can hire boats at Henley, Hurley, Wargrave and Cookham.

The Old Church Hotel

Old Church Hotel
Watermillock, Penrith,
Cumbria CA11 0JN (3m SW of
Pooley Bridge; 6m from M6 –
junction 40).
Telephone: Pooley Bridge (085
36) 204.
DBB B; SBB A.
Some rooms have no private
bathroom.
Dinner B.
Closed November to 2 weeks
before Easter.
No credit cards.

Simple pleasure.

A little gem, in a magnificent position beside the shore of Ullswater lake, second largest in England. The house was built in 1754 on the site of a twelfth-century church. It stands in its own grounds away from traffic, with lawns right down to the lake, and the view of lake and mountains beyond is stunning.

Though it is much simpler than most of the hotels I have chosen, and some rooms have no bathrooms, it has a coveted red star for exceptional merit from the AA, which describes its atmosphere perfectly – 'unaffected warmth and hospitality'.

Kevin Whitemore, the owner, is the chef. His wife Maureen was an interior decorator and her professionalism shows. The dining room is tastefully designed with antique tables, and she has not been afraid to mix oak and mahogany woods or different shapes. Chair covers, carpet and table mats are in Regency green. The bedrooms show the same good taste and willingness to mix good pieces in different styles.

They have no telephones, radio or TV, but many have fine lake views. Ours had big windows. There is TV in one of the comfortable sitting rooms. And there is a small bar. Two large St Bernard dogs add an extra something.

The hotel has moorings, so you can take your own boat, or hire one by prior arrangement. Good windsurfing, too, game and coarse fishing, pony trekking and guided fell walking and rock climbing.

Food & Drink

It will delight not only many of my English readers but Americans, Canadians and Australians, too, to know that Kevin Whitemore offers fine fresh English ingredients cooked in traditional English manner, and that he makes a delicious steak and kidney pie. But he did delight Barbara, whose figure deserves more respect than mine, by offering a lighter dish of local lamb with an untraditional sauce of yoghurt and ginger. Mind you, the Elizabethans used ginger in their sauces. The third choice of main course was pork fillet

Tosca, which means with fennel.

He offers a set menu of four courses, with three choices in each course, which he believes to be the best way of using the freshest possible ingredients cooked absolutely straightaway. The meals are very good value.

He has a fine touch. He can make a cream of spinach soup into a gourmet dish. Barbara followed this with Washington salad (oranges, bananas, strawberries with cream cheese) though the alternative was goujons of really fresh plaice, deep fried. He served plenty of fresh, crispy vegetables,

including little young courgettes and mange-touts. Among the sweets was an excellent mousse of apple and Calvados. They used to make that in Kent many years ago with very old, strong cider instead of Calvados.

Housewines include a German white Qualitätswein, a light dry white Frascati from the hills near Rome, a Bordeaux Rouge, and a red from Chanson, the Beaune négociant. None could be called *plonk*.

Kevin has on his list some very drinkable, not too expensive red Burgundies from the great and reliable Louis Latour

– splendid for that steak and kidney pie, especially the Vignes Franches 1976 from Beâune, a very good year of a very good wine. Or you could choose the Saint-Estèphe claret of Cordier, Château Meyney 1978, still fruity but ready for drinking.

If you like a good strong wine, still fruity, and excellent value here, try the Italian Barolo of the Cavallotto family – Castiglione Fallento. Perhaps it is lucky that Barolo is underestimated outside Italy. Not a lot is produced, and demand could soon push up the price.

There is a dry refreshing ligh Italian white here, best of th Verdicchios – Castelli di Jes Classico. The price is reason able, but it is not for peopl accustomed to white Bur gundy; far too light.

Most wines are also served ir half-bottles.

 LOCAL DRIVES *Passenger boats ply from Glenridding at the foot of Ullswater lake to Pooley Bridge (Easter– mid-October).*

You have the whole Lake District to explore. Get Welcome to English Lakeland from Information Centre, Ambleside, Lake Windermere. You get to the lake (16m) by A592 and the Kirkstone Pass. It is ten and a half miles long. You reach it near Troutbeck. In Troutbeck village is Town End, yeoman farmer's house of 1623 with original furniture, kitchen utensils, books and old fabrics (same family lived there for 300 years). Bowness is the original Windermere village, now a tourist centre. From here (or Lakeside and Ambleside) you can get pleasure cruisers (Easter–September). Boats

also go to Belle Isle, 38-acre island in centre of the lake, with a roundhouse built in 1774, now with portraits by Romney and superb Gillow furniture (open May 15– September 15 except Friday, Saturday).

At the village of Windermere near Bowness is Brockhole National Park Centre and gardens (good audio-visual exhibitions – open late March–early November) and a fascinating unique Steamboat Museum, with world's oldest mechanically-powered boat and trips aboard a 1902 steam launch (open April–Mid-November). At Newby Bridge (bottom of Lake Windermere) is Fell Foot Park (bathing, fishing, rowing, picnics); also terminus of Lake Side and Haverthwaite steam railway (3½m into beautiful scenery of a river valley – open Easter

and May–September). At Ambleside (top of Lake Windermere) is the National Park Information Centre. Also Lake District Heritage Centre (open March 1–October 31).

Outside Ambleside is Rydal Mount, poet William Wordsworth's home from 181 until his death in 1850; contains portraits, personal possessions, first editions; 4-acre gardens landscaped by him (open daily except Wednesday in winter). At Grasmere nearby is Dove Cottage, where Wordsworth lived 1799–1808; many treasures of the poet (open early March–end October).

For Pooley Bridge and Penrith, see Sharrow Bay Hotel, page 144.

For Keswick, Bassenthwaite Lake and Derwent Water, see Underscar Hotel, page 151.

Palé Hall Hotel
Llandderfel, near Bala,
Gwynedd, North Wales
LL23 7PS (5m NE of Bala; turn
left off A494 Chester–Bala
road onto B4401).
Telephone: Llandderfel
(06783) 285.
DBB C–E;
SBB B.
Dinner C (five courses);
lunch A.
No credit cards.

Take someone whom you hope will fall in love with you. Betty Duffyn, the blonde owner, believes that her beautiful house, its grounds and local countryside are the right background for romance. Barbara thinks that picking the romantic suite with a round bed and an invigorating double round jacuzzi bath would help, too. I should rely on the food and Premier Cru clarets.

Newly opened, this sumptuously and tastefully furnished hotel has already made an impact, for Wales is not overstocked with luxurious country hotels.

The Hall was built as a country house 'regardless of expense' in 1870 for a Scots railway engineer who worked with Robert Stephenson and built many lines, including Bala–Ffestiniog. His son was knighted by Queen Victoria, who visited Palé in 1889. The suite in which she slept has a 'half-tester' antique bed and the original bath which she used.

Our most pleasant room had a big bay window, two velvet-covered armchairs, Japanese prints, original sea scene pictures, a bowl of fruit, jar of peppermints, and sherry. In the bathroom was a corner bath, bidet, even bathrobes.

The impressive hall is superbly panelled and has a balconied landing. All the rooms are delightfully furnished, particularly the dining room, which has a beautiful ornate ceiling in green and gold and Italian carved dining chairs upholstered in gold, all reflected in huge original gilt-framed mirrors. The 'boudoir' has a fine hand-painted dome ceiling. The original 1870 cooker is in the breakfast room and the bar is made from old marble fireplaces.

The hotel has a plunge pool with jacuzzi, sauna, sunbed and exercise room.

Food & Drink

The cooking is excellent, the meals fulfilling without being overfilling. Some find the very-reasonably priced five course dinner a little too much, I am told, especially if they choose the soup as second course rather than the sorbet, but I think that they should get out among those mountains, lakes and river walks and work up a bigger appetite. The choice on this set-price meal is almost frustrating. If you could cut down the choice of eight starters to two, you might still take half an hour and a bottle of white wine to decide between marinaded fillets of local trout and a 'duet of seafood pâtés' – salmon and smoked salmon and kipper and malt whisky, served with a few prawns. Then how do you choose a main course between poached local salmon, turbot, sirloin steak, roast duckling, suprême of chicken and roast loin of Welsh lamb, all freshly cooked, looking superb and with individualistic garnishes and sauces, like asparagus cream stuffing and sherry cream sauce with diamond of ham for the chicken and garlic soufflé and tomato and basil sauce for the lamb?

The chef may serve Welsh mountain lamb, lobster and prawns from Shell Island and salmon from the Welsh River Dee but I don't think he is a true Welshman – not with a name like David Atkinson, serving kipper and whisky pâté and lobster Auld Reekie, which is flamed in malt whisky with apple, celery and cream.

There are more excellent dishes on his card, but I would not look past the set-price menu.

Three first growth clarets are expensive but below most hotel prices – Château Margaux 1974 and 1975 and a

Lafite-Rothschild 1970. At the other end of the scale there were (in autumn 1985) many good, drinkable wines at around £6–£7, most of which were being offered at around £10 elsewhere, including such Italian wines as the delicate white dry Verdicchio Dei Castelli di Jesi and a strong, irony he-man's red Bull's Blood from Hungary.

In between, I would go for the Château Phelan Ségur 1975, a red Bordeaux from St Estèphe which is a Grand Cru Bourgeois Exceptionnel, which means it is just about top of the non-classified wines. It is a little light but with a fine flavour. There is also a very pleasant St Emilion 1978, Château La Dominique.

Spanish wines are most interesting and well chosen. There is a good choice of wines from Miguel Torres' Bodegas in Penedes region, in the hills south of Barcelona. Torres is far and away one of the best producers in Spain. The Gran Coronas 1978, a blend of Cabernet Sauvignon and native grapes, is a velvety wine, full of flavour after five years in the bottle and has a violety smell. It is second only to the great Gran Coronas Black Label, which is very difficult indeed to find. From the same Torres Bodegas comes the best white wine in Spain – the dry Gran Vina Sol Green Label, aged in oak, then in bottle, made in small quantities from selected grapes, fresh, fruity with a fine bouquet. In 1985, Palé was offering the 1981 wine for £8.75 a bottle.

There are some of the best Spanish Rioja wines on this

list, too, including a 1978 Reserva from the Domaine of Domecq, the sherry family who have done wonders to improve Rioja winemaking since they moved up to the north of Spain.

Eating and drinking at Palé is a good experience for the palate, stomach and wallet. Go there before the big guides find out about it.

There are lovely walks in the sixteen acres of wooded grounds and beyond. The mountain, woodland, lake and river scenery is magical. On Lake Bala (Llyn Tegid to the Welsh) you can sail, canoe, row, go windsurfing or fish, and you can canoe and shoot rapids on the wild River Tryweryn. The River Dee has superb salmon and coarse fishing. Lake Bala, a mile wide and four and a half miles long, is the largest natural lake in Wales. The gwyniad, white-scaled salmon, lives about eighty feet deep and can be caught only in a net. Steam trains run on a narrow-gauge track from Bala down the lakeside to Llanuwchllyn, home of the Edwards family, champions of the Welsh language. You will find some people here who speak only Welsh. South of Bala, reached best by unclassified mountain roads from the south tip of the lake, is the Arans mountain range. Aran Fawddwy is the highest mountain in Wales outside the Snowdon range.

West from Bala is Blaenau Ffestiniog, where slate quarries still operate. Slate

crags overhang the houses. The narrow gauge Ffestiniog railway (steam) now carries tourists, not slate, to Porthmadoc's harbour, now a holiday centre for watersports and riding.

Following A496 S from Blaenau Ffestiniog you reach Harlech Castle, a magnificent grey stone pile built by Edward I in 1283. Here the wife and family of the Welsh hero Owen Glendower were captured by Henry Tudor, the Welsh King of England Henry V. The song 'Men of Harlech' was written about a Lancastrian who held the castle in the fifteenth-century Wars of the Roses. From Harlech are superb views of the Snowdon Range and the Lleyn Peninsula. Inland, on the Rhinog Mountains nature

reserve, herds of wild goats roam.

Southwards again is Mochras (Shell Island) a strange isle made of sand dunes — formed when in 1819 a landowner diverted a river to steal land from the sea. It is rich in shells, 170 kinds of wild flowers, including several types of orchid and wild dwarf roses, many types of sea and land birds, lobsters, prawns and other shellfish off the banks, and seals.

Barmouth, a seaside resort, has fine walks around. It is also starting point of the odd Three Peaks yacht race in June. Competitors sail to Fort William in Scotland, stopping on the way to run up Snowdon, Scafell Pike and Ben Nevis. Barmouth is joined by ferry to Fairbourne, a little

Victorian resort between hills and dunes with another little steam railway built in 1865 to carry slate, now carrying passengers between end of March and New Year's Day. There is yet another steam railway further south from Tywyn inland, called Talyllyn Railway.

From Barmouth A496 turns E to Dolgellau (Dolgelley when I was young), a little town of narrow streets beside green slopes rising to the craggy summits of Cader Idris, the 2,927-ft peak. It means the chair of Idris — Arthur's seat to us English.

For more information on Snowdonia and the Lleyn Peninsula, see Bodysgallen Hall Hotel, Llandudno, page 21, and Porth Tocyn Hotel, Abersoch, page 124.

PENGETHLEY

Pengethley Hotel
Nr Ross-on-Wye,
Herefordshire HR9 6LL (4m N
of Ross on A49 Hereford road;
6m from M50).
Telephone: Harewood End
(098987) 211.
DBB D–F;
SBB from C.
Many much cheaper mini
breaks.
Dinner C–E.
Open all year.
No bed charge for children
sharing parents' room.
Dogs at management's
discretion.
Credit cards: Euro, Visa,
Amex, Diners.

A captivating place, relaxing but happy and certainly not dull. People I know from seventeen to seventy have been captivated by it.

A fine white house, Georgian now, but partly from 1544, with extra bedrooms in 1544 coach house, it stands in the rolling, fertile hills of Herefordshire, between the Malvern Hills and the Welsh Borders. It is well back from roads in fifteen acres of gardens and grounds, with a swimming pool, a trout lake for fishing, walled garden and orchard, and there are panoramic views across countryside which produces some of the finest food in

Europe from pastures, rivers, streams and woods.

You could easily spend your time lazing, wandering, perhaps fishing, eating and sleeping. Or you can join in the hotel activities. The old stables have been turned into a little entertainment centre with bar and concert room where every Thursday from May to October they have live jazz cabaret and sometimes more classical entertainment. Don't worry – you cannot hear it in the hotel. Many other little excuses are made for celebratory dinners and for wine tastings with dinners to match. Andrew Sime is a lively and caring host – and no mean jazz drummer. There are a large comfortable bar, two lounges and two dining rooms. One, the Nelson, is very attractive, with windows to the sunken garden made from cellars of 1544. It is named after Andrew's great, great, great, great uncle, one *Lord* Nelson.

I think you will love this house, its atmosphere, position and food. The bedrooms recently beautifully refurbished, are excellent but highly

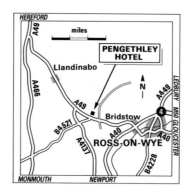

priced. However, if you take a two- or three-day mini-break, with dinner, bed and breakfast, or a longer stay, the cost per day is much lower.

The bathrooms have some splendid touches. On our last visit, we had a spa bath, separate shower cabin, and even two extra towels marked 'swimming pool'.

Food & Drink

Eating and drinking is a great joy at Pengethley. Ian Mann is a very good chef indeed, creative and careful, and he has some wonderful fresh ingredients to help him, and changes the menu regularly to use them, so that he never uses factory or processed frozen foods. Wye salmon, trout from a dozen streams, Ryeland lamb from the hotel's pastures or lamb from Wales, free range poultry and eggs from birds you can see wandering round the back of the hotel, fruit, herbs and vegetables grown in the hotel's walled garden, local beef from Herefordshire cattle (magnificent!), venison and game, and fish delivered regularly from a Cornish trawler. What a world apart from processed foods!

Prices of dinner depend on the main course. His starters always include some imaginative salads, often in walnut oil, and usually smoked chicken and smoked ham dishes. He makes a delicious mousse of Cornish crab, served with a Julienne of fresh ginger and spring onion, with a sauce of soy and dry sherry. Most effective. Barbara tried recently a quail salad with chicory leaves, radish and sliced strawberries, then slices of Wye salmon lightly fried in oil with a sorrel and cream sauce. But I go for any Hereford beef dishes.

The vegetables choice that time was potatoes, new and sautéed with cheese and minced ham, and lightly cooked mange-tous, yellow beans, sliced carrots and courgettes in wine. From a fine list of tempting sweets Barbara chose profiteroles with Tia Maria flavoured cream and caramel sauce. But they grow lovely raspberries and black and red currants to use in sweets.

You are invited to say how you like meat and vegetables cooked, and a vegetarian menu is always available. Besides cooking special dinners for people joining in periodic wine tastings, Ian Mann and Andrew Sime have produced a menu for the Health Education Council which has already won them the Golden Lettuce Award. It is a complete meal, free of added sugar, salt and of fat, with a lot of fibre content.

The wine list has a good reputation in the wine world for quality and range. An excellent choice of cheaper clarets, some fairly young and fruity, others mature wines of Bourgeois growth, such as a 1975 Château du Clos Renon. The fine older clarets are good value. There are some fruity young Beaujolais, too, notably a soft Paul Sapin Fleurie with fine flavour which would go nicely with salmon or lighter meats. And among Burgundies is a notable Nuits St Georges 1979 – Les Vaucrains, vineyards developed by the late Henri Gouges, King of the Nuits.

Among Rhônes is a heavy, powerful and splendid wine to drink with Hereford beef – a Gigondas 1977 from Domaine Saint-Gayan. An interesting Rhône is a 1976 St Joseph, from the right bank of the river opposite Hermitage. Vines are grown up a stake, the wine improving with time more than many Rhône wines.

Other French wines include an excellent value '80 Cahors Chambert, splendid with beef or game, and one Spanish wine is a bargain rich tasting wine from Domecq, the sherry family which has taken over areas of Rioja and improved the table wines substantially.

Among whites, Barbara tried with her salmon and loved the 1983 Savennières Clos de Papillon from Anjou, which she pronounced dry and smooth though usually these wines from Chenin grape are too acid when young and need some time. I have heard of Savennières lasting for 50 years. Andrew's recommendation for drinking with salmon is the Jean Varan Sancerre, and I would not argue, although a lightish red wine goes splendidly, too. For a heavyish, strong flavoured cheap white, try the Australian Rosemount Chardonnay.

Andrew Sime keeps one of the best collections of good half bottles of wine I have seen, including some fine old clarets. Why not have a personal wine-tasting for two?

Hereford (10m NW on A49) is a lovely sleepy mediaeval city astride the river Wye but was once a military base for the English invading Wales and the centre of bloody encounters for 600 years until captured by Cromwell in the 1645 Civil War. The superb cathedral is in a mixture of styles from the eleventh century. It holds many treasures, including a chained library of 1,500 books going back to the ninth century, with the Mappa Mundi, a map of the world drawn in the thirteenth century, and King Stephen's chair, oldest in Britain. See also the narrow mediaeval streets, lovely Georgian buildings, the Old House (timber framed, built 1621 and containing Jacobean furniture), Wye bridge with six arches (built 1490), St John's chapel and museum, formerly belonging to Knights of St John, Bulmer's Museum of Cider (Grimmer road, off A438, story of cider making, closed November–March; plus Age of Steam centre with 'King George V' railway locomotive – weekend openings, but check first). Fine riverside walks in meadows over Wye bridge from Bishop's Palace. One of my favourite small cities. Livestock (Hereford cattle) and general market, in Newmarket Street on Wednesdays; general on Saturdays; butter market daily. Lovely South Wales scenery W from Hereford around Hay-on-Wye.

Ross-on-Wye (4m) planned in seventeenth century by John Kyrle (Pope's Moral Essays – 'Man of Ross'), is still very attractive; see Market Hall (fourteen arches, double gabled, seventeenth century); river Wye from sixteenth-

Trout fishing, wine tasting and jazz in the barn.

century Wilton bridge. At Brockhampton (5m N of Ross off B4224) the church has tapestries by Burne Jones, made in William Morris's workshops; superb thatched lych-gate. At Symond's Yat (5m SW of Ross), the Wye flows round a hill through a narrow gorge in a spectacular five-mile horse-shoe loop nearly joining. A canoeing area. Cave of King Arthur (3m downstream) is where relics of cave-dwellers of 20,000 years ago were found.

Here begins the Forest of Dean – 27,000 acres, mostly oak and beech trees; beautiful drives and walks among hills with fast-flowing streams in valleys. People of the forest have ancient privileges for coalmining (enormous field below forest), cutting stone, grazing sheep. Superb wildlife includes badgers and birds of prey. Speech House, seventeenth-century court house, now part of hotel.

Gloucester (17m E of Ross) – glorious cathedral built by Normans in 1089, beautified by craftsmen in thirteenth century, super tower added in fifteenth century, magnificent fourteenth-century cloisters. Stained glass window 72ft by 38ft is second largest in Britain (the biggest is in York), memorial to the dead at Battle of Crécy in 1346 when the Black Prince defeated the French.

Road south follows Wye valley through Monmouth ruins of castle where Henry V was born in 1387 and fine seventeenth-century Castle House) to Chepstow, with a

Norman castle perched arrogantly on cliffs running steeply down to the Wye estuary; thirteenth-century chapel, graceful old bridge built by John Rennie.

Malvern Hills – see Hope End Hotel, page 65.

Penmere Manor Hotel
Mongleath Road, Falmouth,
Cornwall TR11 4PN.
Telephone: (0326) 314545.
DBB B;
SBB A;
big reductions for children
under 15 sharing parents'
room and 'meals only'
charged in winter.
Dinner A, B;
bar lunch.
Closed December 21–27.
Well-behaved dogs welcome,
but not in public rooms or on
beds.
Credit cards: Euro, Visa,
Amex, Diners.

Penmere Manor is one of those gorgeous white Regency houses which you wish a rich uncle had left you in his will, with enough money to heat it. From the bow windows of the lounge you look downhill across old lawns to five acres of gardens and woodland and from several bedrooms you can see over the trees to the sea in Falmouth Bay. Extensions blend into the old building and the swimming pool nestles discreetly below the lawn.

It is typical of houses built by captains of the Falmouth Packet sailing boats which ran mail and despatches to the West Indies and whose captains grew rich by capturing French boats as 'prizes'. Now it is a very-English style hotel where you feel like a guest at a friend's house. I have met few hoteliers who make you feel as welcome without smothering you as David Pope, his wife Rachel and their daughter Elizabeth Eva, who does the cooking. Great care has been taken with decorations and furnishings to make it look like a comfortable country house –

with a bar! Modest compared with some of my favourites, it is very comfortable and wonderful value.

It is a superb exploring centre. I love Falmouth, the Fal and Helford rivers and the whole area around St Mawes, Portscatho and the Roseland Peninsula. Nowhere else can so evoke the ghosts of past history while remaining a lovely but not rowdy resort. I have only to look from Falmouth across Carrick Roads to imagine the whole stretch of water covered with sailing boats so that you could cross on their decks to the little old port of Flushing or to see the formidable grey Armada of warships, transports, merchantmen, water boats and tankers which gathered here for the D-Day invasion. Now the boats are yachts, fishing boats and a few smaller merchantmen – boats for peace and pleasure.

Lovely gardens and superb sailing where history was made.

Food & Drink

A fresh roast every night. Fresh fish landed by Falmouth trawlers or caught in local rivers or creeks. Steak and kidney pie – one of the world's great dishes. You won't get much raspberry vinegar or fancy patterns on your plate at Penmere, but you will get some of the best of traditional English cooking, using fresh local products. And the menu changes daily. There is always one main fish dish.

I have had splendid John Dory, poached with scallops in wine, good monkfish, that ugly fellow which the French call lotte and regard as such an expensive delicacy, and superb Cornish crab.

I like Elizabeth Eva's soups, too. Last time I had a tasty carrot and orange soup, and the Stilton and spring onion is a favourite.

She makes a different flavoured ice cream each day and other desserts vary from farmhouse pies to light concoctions with Cornish cream. You get a choice of English cheeses for your money, too.

With old English roasts and steak and kidney pies you have a wonderful reason to choose a full-blooded red wine – like the alcoholic, dark, heavy Bull's Blood from Hungary, drunk there by soldiers, horsemen and peasants through the centuries – a bargain here on this fairly modest list of around fifty wines, there are many bargains by most hotels' prices. The dearest wine is a Grand Cru Château Pavie from St Emilion at around £17 – and that is truly one of my favourites. 'Easy to drink', says the list. *Too* easy! There is a very good choice of cheap reds and whites.

There is a fair choice of whites to accompany the fish. The Muscadet at £5.65 is a very crisp Cassemichère, a château owned by one of the biggest dealers and very reliable. The

Chablis is adequate and cheap, the Pouilly-Fuissé is very fruity and cheap for this usually-overpriced wine, but for £14 there is a good Puligny Montrachet, a wine made to drink with fish like monkfish –

rich flavoured but ultimately dry.

I have always thought that the wines of Château de Beauregard, on the borders of Pomerol and St Emilion, deserved more regard, so to speak. They can be

drunk young, smell of fruit and have a lot of flavour. Try the 1983 on this list – and you will see what I mean.

You can eat and drink well at Penmere Manor without going broke.

Mild winters and its suntrap position make Falmouth a town of flowers, shrubs and trees, with sub-tropical plants commonplace. Each time it has entered the Britain in Bloom contest, it has won a major prize. There are beautiful and renowned gardens within driving distance, too. Three miles off the A39 road to Truro (10m from Falmouth) are the National Trust Trelissick gardens in a wooded park by the river Fal, with superb camellias, hydrangeas, rhododendrons and semi-tropical trees. Six miles NE of Truro on A390 is the remarkable County Demonstration Garden at Probus, a Mecca to a dedicated gardener. It is for everyone – home gardener, professionals, architects, planners, housing committees, schools. You can see for yourself how soil conditions, fertilisers, dry, damp, wind

and sea affect plants and trees. It is open May–September, Monday–Friday 10–5, Sunday 2–6; October–April, Monday–Friday 10–4.30, and any Thursday afternoon you can bring sick plants or just blotchy leaves for clinical advice.

In the seventeenth and eighteenth centuries, ships sailed to 'Falmouth for orders'. It was quicker to get orders from London by horse than trying to belt up the Channel under sail. So captains moved their families to Falmouth and Flushing, the little village across the Carrick Roads. On a cliff overlooking the big sand beach and the harbour stands Pendennis Castle, last stronghold of Charles I to fall. It was built by Henry VIII with St Mawes Castle opposite to defend Carrick Roads. The Killigrew family, originally smugglers, built up Falmouth from a village called Pennycomequick (Pen-y-Cum-Cuic –

head of the creek).
One became Governor of the castle and headed a Royal Commission into piracy, then rife off Cornwall. While he was investigating, his own wife ran a pirate fleet!

St Mawes is a delightful, pretty old fishing harbour but crowded in summer. At Mylor, over the peninsula from Flushing, the Navy trained boy entrants in sail and seamanship until recently. Now it is a leisure sailor's little paradise with yards, chandlers, foodstore and restaurant. Its strange old church has a thin spire.

Truro has an attractive 'Early English' style cathedral, built in 1890s and Georgian terraces worthy of Bath.

For Port Navas oyster beds, Helford river and more lovely gardens, see Meudon Hotel, Mawnan Smith, page 98. For St Ives, Penzance and Land's End, see Lamorna Cove Hotel, page 80.

Plumber Manor
Sturminster Newton,
Dorset DT10 2AF
(2m SW on Hazelbury Bryan
road; S of A357; 9m SW of
Shaftesbury).
Telephone: (0258) 72507.
DBB B–C; SBB B.
Menus C
Closed first two weeks of
November and all February;
restaurant closed Mondays
(except for residents April–
October).
No lunches served.
No credit cards accepted.
No children under 12.

*You could only
find it in England!*

A sweeping drive through the farm crosses the Divelish trout stream, then leads under old chestnut trees to the family home since 1665 of the Prideaux-Brunes. They opened a restaurant in it in 1973 and an hotel in 1982, but the two brothers who run it grew up here and it is still home to them and the children. They make friends of their guests. Family portraits line the gallery leading to the bedrooms, which are beautifully furnished with antique heirlooms. The jaunty-looking woman whose portrait is by the stairs is 'great-grandma – an American'. 'Granddad' is in 1914–18 Army uniform. The lovely black-haired girl whose picture in a black evening dress off one shoulder seduced me as I dined is simply 'Grandma'.

A huge stone barn has been made into six delightful, enormous groundfloor bedrooms, plushly and cleverly furnished, overlooking the 15-acre garden and park and another little bridge across the trout stream – a tributary of the river Stour. They have TV but, more important, thick bath-towels big enough to envelop even my girth. All bedrooms have private bathrooms. They are excellent value.

There is a tennis court and croquet lawns, and riding is easily arranged. The atmosphere is relaxed and happy. Richard Prideaux-Brune, the owner, told me: 'We wouldn't do this if we didn't have fun.'

Food & Drink

Chef Brian Prideaux-Brune wears a colourful Scottish Tam o'Shanter. He has a healthy independence from fashions, fads and rigid old rules of cooking.

He has a choice of dishes which change with the seasons and several first and main course 'dishes of the day' which follow the market, such as salmon, asparagus, game. He uses effectively the best of fresh British meat and fish and traditional herbs like thyme, tarragon and sage.

He makes excellent soups, a good strong duck liver pâté

In the Dorset countryside of Thomas Hardy's novels, the manor is ten miles from Milton Abbas, an eighteenth-century model village of white and golden thatched cottages, with a fine eighteenth-century Georgian Gothic church and a mediaeval abbey church restored last century by Sir Gilbert Scott, architect of London's Albert Memorial. The Earl of Dorchester built this village in 1770 after converting the mediaeval abbey into a magnificent house. He had knocked down the old village because he could see it from his windows!

Another lovely village of thatched and Tudor cottages is Cerne Abbas, seven miles north of Dorchester (the Casterbridge of Hardy's novels). On Giant's Hill overlooking Cerne there is cut in the chalky turf the figure of a man 180 ft high wielding a 120-ft knobbly club. It is 1500 years old and was a pagan god of fertility. National Trust.

Sturminster Newton is still an important agricultural market town, with bow-windowed buildings and thatched houses. It has a fine fifteenth-century six-arched bridge over the river Stour which carries a warning of 'Transportation for life' to anyone 'injuring' it and that included driving an overloaded cart on it! North-east of the manor (9m) is Shaftesbury, hilltop town, where Alfred the Great founded a nunnery with his daughter as Abbess. See the steep Gold Hill. South-east of the manor (8m) is Blandford Forum, with a handsome Georgian red-brick and stone centre planned and built after a huge fire in 1731.

The biggest architectural feast is in Sherborne, twelve miles west. Built mainly in golden stone, it is still rich in mediaeval buildings and history. It has a fifteenth-century abbey church which evolved from a cathedral founded in 705AD, and where two Saxon kings, Ethelbald (860) and Ethelbert (866) were buried. An old castle is in ruins, the 'new' one was built by Sir Walter Raleigh. The grounds and lake were laid out by Capability Brown. At Blandford Camp (2 miles NE of Blandford) is the Royal Corps of Signals museum.

with apple purée and almonds and smoked salmon paupiettes filled with smoked trout mousse.

Last time I was there the dishes of the day included first-of-season asparagus, hot crab gratinée, a tasty veal and vegetable terrine in a light curry sauce (I tasted it) and, my choice, four delicious light mousses of fish looking pretty in a lake of vivid green cucumber sauce – salmon, smoked salmon, trout and Arbroath smokies. I denied myself pigeon breasts in blackcurrant and cassis, stuffed suprême of chicken with calvados and apple and poached salmon to choose one of the chef's specialities – escalope of English pasture-fed veal with Parma ham, sage and a delicious creamy Marsala sauce, not too heavy in Marsala. Four vegetables were fresh, plentiful, and cooked crisp but not 'Nouvelle' raw. They included crispy round French beans.

One of his most successful dishes is Beef Wellington – that delicious filling dish of fillet steak in pastry. Another in season is peppered venison steak, with black cherries and cinnamon.

The sweet trolley selection is inevitably rich in confection with clotted Dorset cream. had a delightful strawberr cake made with fresh youn local strawberries, the flakiest lightest of pastries, layered with whipped cream, and clot ted cream alongside. Plumbe Manor is not for slimmers though there are some goo local walks by riversides an across pastures.

Coffee and mints are include in the menu price.

A sensible selection of wine at fair prices includes fou 'carafe quality' French wines £5.50 (1985 price), including crisp, quite fruity dry whit called Clochemerle Blanc. Fo a little more you can try a goo dry white Sauvignon fro Côtes de Duras, an area south Bergerac rather over-shadowe

by its neighbours of Bordeaux, and a pleasant red Montague St Emilion – near neighbour of St Emilion, very drinkable though not so warm or fruity as the real thing.

As a dry white I would have chosen the palatable Pouilly Fumé 'Moulin à Vent' with my fish mousses – not too smokey, reasonably fruity. But I spotted a white I have not tasted for years – Marcel Vincent's Pouilly-Fuissé from Château Fuissé itself. Burgundy is dear these days, particularly Pouilly-Fuissé which has a huge US following, and my half bottle was costly, but I did enjoy it. Once in the mood, I went pedigree-spotting and spent as much on a half bottle of Graves, a 1973 from the Eschenauer vineyard of Château Smith-Haut-Lafitte, which had aged well, was just ready for drinking, with a balance of fruit and tannin.

Several good, pricier wines are on this list at below the cost in many other restaurants. Some lower priced wines are good value, too. With game or Beef Wellington you could drink the 1978 Chianti Classico Riserva from Barone Ricasoli's Brolio Castello. The Ricasoli family has sent wines to Britain since 1604. It is fashionable to decry the wines a little since Seagram Distillers joined the operation. But I can still drink them most happily.

Plumber Manor's restaurant is deservedly popular in the West. The gracious, tasteful dining room adds considerably to the pleasure of eating there.

Porth Tocyn

**Porth Tocyn Hotel
Bwlchtocyn, Abersoch,
Pwllheli, Gwynedd LL53 7BU
(2½m past Abersoch through
hamlets of Sarn Bach and
Bwlchtocyn. Take Sarn Bach
road and follow three signs
marked 'Gwesty/Hotel').
Telephone: Abersoch (075
881) 2966.
DBB B–C;
SBB A.
Dinner C (5 course).
Closed November – just before
Easter.
Credit cards: Euro, Amex.**

Here is Wales' answer to those who have called it 'a gastronomic desert devoid of good hostelries'. Not a luxurious hotel but a relaxed country cottage hotel in a lovely position, serving hearty meals cooked well enough to earn an AA rosette, the approval of Ronay and the Good Food Guide's tireless correspondents and, more important, of its own guests. They return regularly, even over 25 years.

The Fletcher Brewer family made it into an hotel in 1949. 'It was grandmother's hobby,' says grandson Nick, who now runs it with his mother Barbara and his wife. 'Our attachment to it is very deep and we love our work.'

It is at the 'end of the world,' down a maze of narrow lanes on the Lleyn peninsula, with truly splendid views across Tremadog Bay to Snowdonia. It is surrounded by gardens and its own 25-acre farm and is the place to hide someone you love in peaceful seclusion, away from jealous rivals or close-sticking friends.

The house was made from a row of lead-miners' cottages, and although improved each year it keeps its character. Five small lounges lead into each other, furnished with old wood, flowery chintz-covered armchairs, prints and water-colours, ornamental china plates, pottery jugs, lots of magazines, books and flowers. There is a large bar. The delightful panelled dining room, with views across the Bay, has a big old Welsh dresser, antique tables of different shapes and sizes, and chairs of many styles. It has a pleasant air of informality.

Pretty bedrooms are furnished with antiques – comfortable rather than luxurious but all with their own bathrooms and TV. Most have lovely views.

The heated swimming pool is sheltered by bushes and trees. There is a hard tennis court.

Good cooking, excellent value.

Food & Drink

'Cuisine is the backbone of Porth Tocyn's reputation,' says Nick Fletcher Brewer and that reputation seems safe enough at present. The family work with a team of Cordon Bleu cooks, they have set-price meals only, with a fair choice and very good value for five courses. If you have lost your appetite, you can pay less for just two courses and coffee.

We can thoroughly recommend the freshness of ingredients and the cooking. Soups are usually excellent. Salmon, shellfish and white fish are caught locally, and Welsh mountain lamb is delicious.

It is difficult to recommend individual dishes because the whole menu changes daily. I can tell you what was offered at our last dinner.

From four starters, we chose smoked duck with chicory peach salad. Our neighbours raved about the seafood crumble. The soup was Chesterfield – made of mushrooms, celery and onion, creamed with sherry. For the main course we had beautiful poached salmon Veronique (cream sauce with grapes). With it were served green beans in hollandaise sauce, turnips in parsley sauce, and new potatoes.

Barbara, the dessert expert, chose something called Banana Banoffi pie, which she described as a sort of banana cheesecake with caramel. Except in the line of duty, I settle for sorbet in a big meal like this. Diners at another table were in raptures about the whisky bread and butter pudding. Obviously they were greater trenchermen than us. I could not spot a Welsh cheese on the board, not even Caerphilly, but there was a nice, well-kept Derby.

Nick liked a description of his wine list as 'workmanlike'. In a small hotel like this, with most reasonable prices, you do not expect a grand hotel list. But this one is skilfully chosen, with something to please most palates and wallets. Prices are below average, too. There is a cheap housewine at about £2 below the average – a good Muscadet; also a very good value house claret.

Most wines are French or German, with two really good Germans – an Auslese Riesling and a 1971 Beerenauslese Niersteiner Silvaner. Beware of the Johannisberger Riesling – it was Hitler's favourite wine, and Bismarck and Disraeli drank to 'eternal peace' in it – and you know how peaceful Bismarck was!

Among red Bordeaux is the only fifth growth St Estèphe, a 1974 Clos Labory, which is good, not overpriced, and tastes younger than it is, which does no harm. Although it costs over £20, I think that the 1967 Château Cantermerle is something of a bargain. Not all 1967 clarets were mediocre and this fifth growth Macau is rather like a much higher graded Margaux but fuller.

Among cheaper red wines, I would try the 1981 Rully – a Burgundy which we do not often see here – we see more of the white, especially made into excellent sparkling Burgundy by the Champagne method. But the red is improving and with most Burgundies shooting up in price, is well worth drinking. Workmanlike, perhaps?

There are two Torres Spanish wines from Penedes, inland from Tarragona – Vina Sol and the excellent Gran Coronas.

Far grander is the Burgundy Latricières-Chambertin. I have not drunk one for years. These double-barrelled Chambertins, like Gevrey, Charmes, Mazis, Griotte, can be confusing. But this is ranked with Chambertin itself.

 *Nearest sand beach is ten minutes walk. Abersoch is an attractive yachting and power-boat centre, with old stone cottages by the water, a tidal harbour for small boats, and anchorage in St Tudwal's Road for beautiful yachts and cruisers in the lee of St Tudwal's Islands (privately owned). It has a mile-long sand beach backed by dunes, golf course and tiers of holiday chalets. Palms grow on south slopes, as in Cornwall. The Lleyn Peninsula is one of my favourite parts of Britain.*

Rocky coves, wide bays, enticing sand beaches (26 of them) and headlands with distant views of mountains, fishing villages and little whitewashed cottages. Westward along the coast from Abersoch is the long curving crescent of Porth Neigwl Bay (Hell's Mouth) with sand and cliffs. A steep and difficult footpath goes to the beach, safe in calm weather. Surfing for strong swimmers in windier times. Strong tides and eddies have wrecked many ships.

Aberdaron is a tiny fishing village with one and a half miles of sand sheltered from all but south winds. At Aberdaron you can hire boats for off-shore fishing or cruising round Bardsey Island.

Right up the northern coast of the peninsula is a succession of small coves with sandy beaches and rock pools, reached by narrow lanes and tracks.

North-east from Abersoch, A499 leads to Pwllheli, biggest town on Lleyn, with a street market on Wednesday held since 1355. The inner harbour has silted up but a few fishing boats, yachts and sailing dinghies use the outer harbour. East of the harbour is a beach with four miles of sand. A modern resort has been built onto the old town.

Criccieth is now a small seaside resort with sand and shingle beaches. Its ruined castle, built in 1230 by the Welsh, is steeped in Welsh history. Edward I took it in 1282 and incorporated it in his defence scheme against Welsh nationalists. The Welsh

hero Owen Glendower took it back in 1404. Magnificent setting on high headland. Nearby at Llanystumdwy, Lloyd George, British prime minister, 1916–22, was brought up. He was known as the Welsh Wizard for his spell-binding oratory. He was buried there in 1945 and a bronze bust stands outside a museum devoted to him.

Porthmadog and Tremadog towns, at the mouth of the Glaslyn river, were started in the nineteenth century by a local MP, William Madocks, who reclaimed land from the mudflats. The picturesque Porthmadog harbour, once used for loading slate, is now used by yachts and sailing dinghies and the old ketch 'Garlandstone' is berthed there as a maritime museum. Centre for canoeing, sailing, fishing, rock-climbing. Two delightful sandy beaches, from one of which a Welsh Prince Madoc is said in old poems to have sailed to America in the twelfth century. T. E. Lawrence (Lawrence of Arabia) was born at Tremadog.

Portmeirion, round the cove, was built in the 1920s by architect Clough Williams-Ellis because he adored Portofino, the Mediterranean fishing village. It has Italianate houses, castles and campanile, sculptures and gardens mixed with architectural oddments from all over Britain. Unfortunately the hotel was burned down in 1981 but is being rebuilt.

For information on Snowdonia and the rest of North Wales, see Bodysgallen Hall, Llandudno, page 21, and Palé Hall Hotel, Bala, page 111.

Prestbury Country House Hotel

Prestbury
Country House Hotel
Brimley Lane, Bovey Tracey,
South Devon TQ13 9JS.
Telephone: (0626) 833246.
DBB B.
Menu (dinner only) A
(5 course).
Closed November, December,
January, February.
No children under 12.
No dogs.
Credit cards:
Euro, Visa,
Amex,
Diners.

Dartmoor has a hundred faces from sinister to smiling. I do not know a more agreeable place from which to explore it in any of its moods than this intimate little hotel.

Prestbury Hotel is just inside the Dartmoor National Park, on the edge of Bovey Tracey, called Gateway to the Moors. You can see in a flash that it is Edwardian – higgledy-piggledy mixture of styles, with some stone mullion windows, half-timbering for decoration, bay windows added as an afterthought, yet all making a harmonious whole. It is a house for living in. Whether taking tea beside the big log fire in the comfortable and elegant main lounge or sitting in the shade of the porch looking across the trim old lawns, shrubs and interesting trees to the wooded moorland slopes beyond and sipping a cool white wine served on a real silver salver, you feel relaxed, at home and cushioned from the noise, buffeting and

smells of the world outside.

There are three lounges, one with TV, the main lounge with sink-in settees and armchairs and a grand piano, and a sun lounge with, surprisingly, a modern electric organ. The owner, John Steventon, has played the organ most of his life. Much of the antique furniture is from his lifetime collection; so are the fine pictures and delightful china ornaments downstairs, on the sweeping staircase and galleried landing, and in the bedrooms. John and Barbara Steventon were both in the pottery business in Stoke. All bedrooms are different and pleasant.

Long ago, the two-acre garden was cunningly laid-out, with open slopes to show the view and secretive arbors of little lawns behind trees and shrubs.

The welcome in this little hotel is absolutely genuine, the service gracious. In three years the Steventons have already won the coveted HBL award from the AA for hospitality and comfortable bedrooms and lounges, a BTA recommendation, and a spot in Michelin.

A serene English country home and garden in wild Dartmoor.

Food & Drink

John and Barbara Steventon share the cooking and are so atuned that if one is interrupted while making a dish, the other can take over. They are devoted to fresh local food, except for lamb, which they have delivered from the Welsh mountains. They use Devon beef, salmon and trout from the river Dart, venison from Dartmoor, poultry from free-range local farms, Devon cream and butter direct from farms, crab and white fish from the Brixham fishing fleet on the nearby coast. Salmon, chicken, goose and duck are smoked locally.

It is almost their hobby to find English farm cheeses: Sharpham, looking like a Brie, but with a distinctive flavour of the irony red Devon soil; Beenleigh blue, a local ewes' milk cheese, and a goats' milk from the same

maker; truckle cheddar, Cornish Yarg rolled in nettles from Liskeard, and occasionally a *genuine* Dorset Blue Vinney.

There is a set dinner with a choice of four dishes on each of five courses. It is splendid value – the best of English cooking of fine fresh ingredients.

Last time I chose devilled Brixham crab, then sautéed lamb's liver in a home-made crab apple jelly. The liver was delicious – sliced thin, succulent and cooked almost to perfection. The vegetables were new potatoes, buttered fresh green beans and cauliflower with almonds.

On the sweet trolley were Barbara Steventon's very special coffee gâteau, orange sorbet served in orange shells with Cointreau, Bakewell tarts and, my choice, Devon junket, served with Devon cream and two big blobs of clotted Devon cream, too. John is free with

clotted cream unless you tell him that you are slimming, whereupon he shrugs and says: 'We are only here once, you know.'

The splendid cheese board followed, then coffee. The cost is incredibly low. Another time I had locally-smoked fillet of goose breast to start, then a delicious ragout of venison.

Wines are modest and very reasonably priced indeed. You have a choice of four very cheap housewines including a quaffable Cherancay dry white and (much less to my taste) a Hallgarten Kellergeist. A La Cassemichère Muscadet which I drank with the devilled crab cost me little more. With the liver I had a Louis Jadot 1979 Côtes de Beaune Villages. I could have chosen a 1978 Marqués de Riscal Spanish Rioja or a 1982 Mouton Cadet Rothschild, at rock-bottom prices. Louis Lussac Côtes de Rhône for £4.70 (1985) sounds like old times. But I would have liked the choice of a couple of better clarets on the list, like a premier cru St Emilion and a middle-grade Margaux.

To accompany those delicious dishes from local ingredients, you could choose an English wine – a Müller-Thurgau white from the Whitstone vineyards of the Barclays – just down the road, at Bovey Tracey! It travels the two miles very well . . .

 Dartmoor National Park covers 365 square miles, of which unfortunately forty square miles are leased by the Army for training. Forty per cent of the Moor is Commonland, privately owned but it may not be fenced in and there are common grazing rights for local farmers. They own the sheep, cattle and the famous Dartmoor ponies which you see grazing. Here you can get further from habited houses than anywhere in Southern England. Set on a plateau around 1,000 feet high, mostly of granite covered with peat, some of it treeless and uncultivated. Tors (peaks) rise from it. The highest (2,039ft) is High Willhays, but it is in the military zone. Haytor (1,490ft) five miles west of Bovey on the Widecombe road, has views on fine days to the coast. Bovey has granite houses with thatched roofs. Parke, a 200 acre woodland estate, in Haytor road, is a rare-breeds farm with long-horned cattle, old-fashioned sheep, pigs and brightly-coloured poultry which farmers bred in the Middle Ages (open April 1– October 31; also Park headquarters for information).

Among interesting sights on Dartmoor are Lydford Gorge (National Trust), between Tavistock and Okehampton 100ft White Lady waterfall and Devil's Cauldron). See also Buckfast Abbey (historic abbey founded by King Canute, suppressed by Henry VIII in 1535, revived by refugee French monks in the nineteenth century). It has a 1932 church in pure white Bath stone and a chapel with colourful stained glass walls.

Buckland Abbey (converted into a house by Sir Richard Grenville, naval commander and privateer cousin of Sir Walter Raleigh, who sold it to Sir Francis Drake) has scale models of ships from ancient times to today, murals of Drake's voyage round the world, a Devon crafts gallery and, in the great Banqueting Hall, Drake's Drum; when England is in danger, we must beat the drum and then, as Drake promises in Henry Newbolt's poem, 'If the Dons sight Devon, I'll quit the port of Heaven and drum them up the Channel, as we drummed them long ago'. Widecombe: amid a cluster of white cottages is the tall church tower, a moorland landmark of the village to which, in the old song, Uncle Tom Cobleigh and his friends took Tom Pearse's grey mare.

Postbridge has a thirteenth-century clapper bridge of granite slabs weighing up to eight tons each on tall piles above the East Dart River. Two Bridges also has a mediaeval clapper bridge. Buckland-in-the-Moor (SW of Bovey) is a photographer's dream village, with thatched granite houses in a wooded dale. Chagford is a pretty old market town with good views, quaint houses, and old inns round the market square. Dartmoor prison is at Princetown, the ugliest part of the moor, so don't bother unless interested in history or the macabre. It was built to imprison the French captured in the Napoleonic wars in 1809, and in 1813 2,000 American sailors captured during sea encounters were confined there for two years. At the market town of Buckfastleigh you can take a steam train for seven miles beside the river Dart (closed September–Easter). Engine sheds here contain locomotives and stock; also a miniature steam railway.

Torquay, sophisticated and elegant seaside resort and famous yachting centre where the Olympic races were held, is twelve miles from Prestbury Hotel. At High Blagden (3m W of Torquay) is Torbay Aircraft Museum with planes old and newer, the original Colditz glider built by RAF PoWs for escapes, model railway, period costumes, and rose garden dedicated to actor Kenneth More. Also Brixham, superb old fishing port.

Exeter is 15½ miles (see Woodhayes Hotel, Whimple, page 160).

The Priory

**The Priory Country House
Hotel
Rushlake Green,
Heathfield, East Sussex,
TN21 9RG
(S of B2096
Heathfield-Battle road, turn
off at Three Cups Corner).
Telephone: (0435) 830553.
DBB C–E; SBB C
Set lunch A;
4-course dinner C.
Closed mid-December–mid-
January.
No children under 9.
No credit cards.**

A place to find peace, friendliness, fine food, excellent wine, in the heart of the Sussex countryside, within 100 acres of farmland, copses and rough land rich in wildlife. Take walking shoes and someone who likes ambling.

Peter Dunn and his wife Jane, an interior designer, converted a 500-year-old farmhouse on their estate into a true country house hotel when the tenant farmer moved out. Over three years they restored and modernised it with an understanding of its past, and using oaks from their own land for timber.

It has belonged to their family

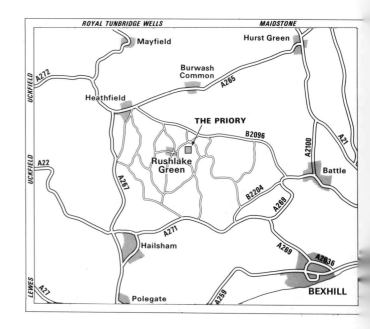

or 400 years and they still have Henry VIII's original Deed of Grant. It was built in 1412 as a Priory by Augustinian monks from nearby Hastings. When Henry VIII dissolved the monasteries, he gave it to his Attorney-General, Sir John Baker, who sold it to the Dunns' ancestors. When converting, they found the ruins of the Priory chapel and the spring from which the monks drew water.

In the original farmhouse hallway are nostalgic pictures of farmers and their families with decorated carts, one-family cricket teams, harvest scenes and sons in uniform in the Kaiser's war. Now you enter the rambling building of weathered stone and timber up

steps from the fine old garden into a beamed lounge with soft padded armchairs and a huge fireplace burning logs in winter. Beyond is another lounge as big and comfortable. Bedrooms vary in size but they nearly all have old beams, all have bathrooms and colour TV and are centrally heated. They are furnished with care and provided with almost everything you might need, from hot water bottles, clothes brush and sewing kits to books and tempting biscuits. The drapes are bright and sunny.

There are pleasant walks around the garden and beyond, fishing in a stream and shooting in season. It is warm, cosy and invigorating in winter, relaxing in summer.

Food & Drink

Meals at the Priory show what can be done with fairly simple but imaginative cooking of fresh local food. I really enjoy eating here. It is rich farming country, famous for lamb, with much local game in season, especially pheasant, plenty of fruit from nearby Kent, trout from local streams, and excellent fresh fish landed daily at Hastings, 15 miles away.

Between them, Jane Dunn and Sharon Winter have some bright ideas in the kitchen. Dishes follow seasons but you get plenty of choice. Last time as a starter there was potted rabbit, made with marinated rabbit set with plums in a fruit and port aspic. Or you could have mushrooms and garlic baked with slightly-sour cream and cheese, or pancakes with fennel, lemon, prawns and smoked salmon gratinée with cheese, sautéed calves liver in salad, a soup of mussels and vegetables, or a terrine of garden vegetables set with eggs and cream, served with a creamy cheese sauce. But I chose a light, very tasty but delicate mousse of tomato, Stilton and avocado, served with sauce and cheese pastry. It was delicious. So was Barbara's pancake.

Fresh salmon with cucumber and hollandaise sauce was a main course choice; also escalope of pork surrounded by fruit with an apple and banana sauce, saddle of venison in chunks with a port sauce; a scallop mousse with King prawns in a creamy watercress sauce; boned baby chicken stuffed with veal sweetbread, ham and mushrooms in a wine sauce, and sautéed fillet of beef with creamy tomato and spinach sauces.

Barbara chose breast of duck, served with lime, sage and red-pepper jelly and a lime and vermouth sauce. But this is lamb country, there is no lamb better than English and Welsh, and I chose best-end, boned, rolled, stuffed with liver, rosemary and walnut, baked to succulent perfection and served with rosemary and Madeira sauce. It was superb. So much for those sneering stories of English country cooking.

The choice of sweets was good, too, including a home-made lemon curd tart; a chocolate marquise made with lime buttercream and with a fresh lime crème anglaise; figs poached in red wine and cointreau, or three different sorbets served on brandy snaps.

The cheeseboard that followed is the pride of the Dunns. Cheese *table*, I should say. On it are more than thirty fresh farm British cheeses, some of which I have not tasted for years. There are local Sussex goats' cheeses made with chives or horseradish or pepper and garlic, a Wharfedale blue goats' cheese, Blue Wensleydale, Red Windsor, Devon Garland, Wartleigh Plain and Beenleigh Blue sheep's cheeses, Double Gloucester with chives (which I have always called Cotswold), Panyllyn goat and a gorgeous farm-made Lancashire.

It is worth going back to the Priory just for the cheeses.

The wines have been chosen by Master of Wine Nicholas Clarke, and mostly come from small local merchants and importers. The list aims to suit as many tastes as possible and is very interesting to a great wine consumer like me. It is also a little frustrating. Will someone please buy me a bottle of the great Bordeaux vintage year 1966 premier cru Château Latour? It will only cost you £99 – plus VAT! And that is frustrating, too – quoting prices on the hotel list 'excluding VAT'.

But it is a lovely list for any one willing to pay over £20 for a bottle and there are some well-chosen wines cheaper like a Charles Pax 1978 heavyish Gigondas for drinking with the lamb, beef or venison, and 1980 Marques de Riscal from the Spanish Rioja. Mr Clarke says that the best *value* in France at present is in Loire and Rhône wines, but he has a lovely list of white Burgundies, including a nice Vaillons premier cru Chablis 1980 from Domaine la Jourchère, a producer new to me. Most people prefer white Burgundies 3 to 5 years old, after which they can lose some freshness, but I am happy with older wines, even of Macon, and there are two real bargains here – a 1973 and 1979 Domaine de la Bon Grain from Jean Thevenet at just over £10.

House wines are good, especially the dry white La Borie, a Loire wine, full and more mellow than cheaper Muscadet.

There is a wide choice of half bottles.

Heathfield (4½m NW) is a pretty old market town with modern extension. It still has two windmills. Its parish church is mostly thirteenth century, with a tower of chalk faced with sandstone. In 1607 the vicar, Roger Hunt, went with colonists to Chesapeake Bay, Virginia, to establish the first permanent English settlement. A church window shows him administering holy communion to colonists, with Indians looking on.

Herstmonceux (5m S): not pretty but interesting. They make trugs – open wooden baskets made of broad bands of willow on a wooden frame. An attractive fifteenth-century castle now houses the Royal Greenwich Observatory, with the conspicuous Isaac Newton Telescope building in its park. Open at advertised times). You can visit the castle grounds but not the building.

Battle (9m SE of Priory Country House) was the scene of the so-called Battle of Hastings in 1066. Here William and his invading Normans played their trick of pretending to flee and then defeated Harold's Saxons who chased them too carelessly. The massive gatehouse remains of the Abbey which William built. In the Langton House museum is a half-size copy (made in 1821) of the Bayeux Tapestry showing the battle.

Hastings (15m SE), a slightly run-down seaside resort, has an attractive old fishing town with an active fishing fleet, tall huts used to dry nets back to Elizabethan days, a thirteenth-century castle reached by lift up the cliffs and a fisherman's museum with an old sailing lugger. In White Rock Pavilion is a modern tapestry 243ft long made by the Royal School of Needlework depicting in 81 scenes events in British history from 1066 until today.

Eastbourne (16m S) was designed in 1834 for the Duke of Devonshire and is still an elegant resort known for flowers, theatre, and tennis championships. Beachy Head is a 534-ft clifftop over the sea with fine views.

Brighton (27m SW) used to be a fishing village, and was adopted in 1783 by the Prince of Wales, son of George III and the future George IV, who made it into the most fashionable resort in Britain and left behind its Regency houses and its fascinating extravagant Royal Pavilion. It is still one of the liveliest, most interesting and sophisticated resorts in Europe.

Nearer to the Priory Hotel is Glynde (15m SW), the village where the famous black-faced Southdown sheep were first bred; it has Glynde Place with a collection of pictures, bronzes and needlework, and nearby is Glyndebourne Opera House, added to a Tudor mansion in 1934. From May until August great singers and conductors perform. Performances begin before 6pm and the 75 minute supper break is a ritual – picnics on the lawn amid lovely gardens, with hampers of fine foods and wines. The Priory will provide them for their guests, with Champagne, of course.

At Burwash (10m N) is Bateman's, a stone mansion with towering chimneys where Rudyard Kipling lived from 1902 until he died in 1936. Here he wrote Puck of Pook's Hill, the poem If and many others. The house was built in 1604. It is now owned by the National Trust and you can visit it. Kipling's study is kept as it was when he used it, including a littered desk 10ft long.

The best of English country cooking – modern style.

The Regent

Regent Hotel
The Parade,
Royal Leamington Spa,
Warwickshire CV32 4AX
(in town centre).
Telephone: (0926) 27231.
DBB C;
SBB A, B;
cheaper short breaks.
Dinner A;
also gourmet Vaults
restaurant card;
lunch A.
Open all year.
Credit cards: Euro, Visa,
Amex, Diners.

Pure Regency. A big white Regency building in a Regency spa. Inside, elegance, grace and a touch of Regency flourish. Many of the world's famous men and women have stayed here – Queen Victoria as a young princess (she later dubbed Leamington 'Royal'), the Duke of Wellington, Napoleon III and the Empress Eugènie, Ulysses Grant (president of the US), Gladstone (four times prime minister), Winston Churchill, Brunel the bridge and railway builder, Charles Dickens, the American poet Longfellow, Ellen Terry, Sarah Bernhardt, film heart-throb Ramon Novarro, Douglas Fairbanks, and C. S. Rolls of Rolls-Royce. These and many more appear on a heritage panel in the hotel and some look down on you from pictures on the great Regency staircase, with its stained glass window of the royal arms, the Prince of Wales feathers and the motto *Ich Dien* – 'I serve', which George IV when Regent and Prince of Wales gave the hotel the right to use.

It is quite different from most of my other choices. It is in a town, though in a fine street. It has eighty bedrooms, and when it was built in 1819 it was the biggest hotel in Europe! It is very comfortable rather than luxurious but has style and atmosphere, with a superb Regency dining room and delightful lounge with fine Regency wall and ceiling decorations. Some bedrooms are in the style, too; some are more modern.

Once we had an enormously wide bed. My old friend Vernon May, manager here for thirty years, believes that people should really enjoy bedrooms. He runs Night to Remember visits, with Champagne, flowers and fruit awaiting you in the bedrooms, gourmet dinner and breakfast in bed any time until noon.

The Cridlan family have owned this hotel since 1904 and they have made it rather a centre of the town, many things to many people. Apart from the Regency dining room, one bar called Cork and Fork has table seating to serve food rather fast and in the vaults is a restaurant

where more ambitious dinners are served. There is a ballroom with dancing every Friday to live music. Leamington is a charming and lovely little town, with a casino and pump room, and it's a good centre for seeing many places of interest.

Food & Drink

Cooking at the Regent is an upstairs, downstairs affair. The very experienced head chef, Mattia Garguilo, looks after the main Regency Chandos restaurant, where the fixed price lunches and dinners are outstanding value. Down in the

vaults young Roland Clark also has a good value set lunch and dinner à la carte with fine old-fashioned English cooking, excellently executed.

The upstairs lunch has plenty of choice, with a main course of such dishes as steak, kidney and mushroom pie, roast lamb, duck in orange sauce, grilled trout. At dinner the starters might include creamed sweetbreads in Cointreau, smoked pork with scrambled eggs and Stilton, and Armagnac pâté, the main courses poached salmon, lambs' kidneys in Madeira, salmis of pheasant and grilled steak. All straightforward dishes, carefully

cooked and in good portions.

It is much the same in the Vaults – a card with plenty of choice, which does not look very exciting or inventive, but from which I have had really excellent traditional meals of top-quality fresh products with finely-made sauces. With prime best end of neck of lamb (one of my favourite meats) is served a tasty but not overpowering sauce of port, orange and redcurrant – not quite a Cumberland sauce, which might be too strong for the lamb's fairly delicate flavour. Fillet of beef is pan fried with six different herbs.

Roland Clark makes good old-

fashioned Crêpes Suzette – one of the few dishes which break my personal rule that cooking should be done in the kitchen, not on the dining table.

If you want modern French cooking, you will be disappointed at the Regent. It is for traditionalists wanting the best of old-style British.

The 'small' wines on the list, like Appellation Controlée Beaujolais and Fleurie, Muscadet, Pinot Blanc Alsatian, Sancerre, Spanish Rioja and a first growth Chablis are all excellent value for money. You could, of course, pay £200 a bottle for one of three gorgeous 1961 wines – Château Latour, Mouton Rothschild and Margaux. I would not drink the stuff – unless some rich man insisted on paying for it! Even then, I think I would sooner have six bottles of the 1966 Rausan Segla Margaux. A terrible thought for mature wine drinkers like me – 1961 seems like only yesterday!

In truth, with the roasts and

beef dishes I would certainly go for the cheap Côte de Blaye 1979, Côtes de Plaisance. Blaye is a charming, fruity Bordeaux 'just right for drinking every day', as a certain mayor of Bordeaux told me. In the medium range, one wine stands' out – Château Leoville Barton 1977. The wine was a little lighter than usual that year, which may account for its comparatively low price, but it is still delightfully fruity and tempting. I am one of those dedicated consumers who believe that nothing very bad ever comes out of St Julien. When in doubt, aim for it. And this is a second growth, not all that much below the great first growth wines of Lafite and Haut Brion.

One of our most historic hotels.

At Stoneleigh (3m N) is the National Agricultural Centre, with the Royal Show Ground and equestrian centre of the British Show Jumping Association. It is in the grounds of Stoneleigh Abbey, a twelfth-century abbey founded by Henry II, later blended with a Georgian house. The River Avon flows by the original gatehouse. Most attractive village with an ancient 9-arch bridge, an eighteenth-century bridge, lovely old cottages and a smithy by the village green.

The National Exhibition Centre is near Birmingham airport, fourteen miles away. Stratford-on-Avon is ten miles (see Billesley Manor Hotel, page 14).

Warwick Castle (2m) is one of Europe's greatest fortresses. Its sinister but majestic walls and turrets rise above the tree-lined river Avon, hiding a seventeenth-century interior of baronial splendour with magnificent state rooms, a silver vault, ghost tower and a torture chamber. It was the seat of the Earls of Warwick for nearly 1,000 years until the present Earl sold it in 1978 to Madame Tussauds. Some of the family treasures have gone, including great paintings, such as the Canalettos, but there is plenty still to see, including superb tapestries and arms from the Middle Ages to the seventeenth century. And a lot more to see in Warwick, too,

despite a disastrous fire in 1694 which at least made room for fine Georgian houses alongside the timber-framed buildings which escaped. Best of these is Lord Leycester Hospital, for 400 years an almshouse for crippled soldiers. Part of St Mary's Church survived, too. In Beauchamp Chapel is the tomb of Elizabeth I's favourite, the Earl of Leicester. In the mediaeval Elizabeth Oken's house is a museum of dolls and in seventeenth-century St John's House a museum of crafts, costumes and furniture.

Kenilworth (A452 4m N of Leamington) has the dramatic ruins of the great castle on a gentle grass slope. A stronghold for kings and lords in the eleventh and twelfth centuries made into a palace by John o'Gaunt in the fourteenth century. The Earl of Leicester entertained his Royal mistress Elizabeth I here with with a floating artificial island on the lake and a party so lavish that he went bankrupt. Walter Scott's novel Kenilworth is set here.

Coventry is 9m N. The city's most famous citizen Lady Godiva has a statue in Broadgate. She rode naked through the streets to protest against the heavy taxation of her people by her husband, Leofric, eleventh-century Earl of Mercia. Peeping Tom, who looked, gets two statues and a head popping out of a clock. The city's magnificent Phoenix is the new cathedral, designed by Sir Basil Spence

and one of Europe's finest examples of modern architecture. On a night in November 1940 Hitler's bombers destroyed forty acres of the city centre, including the cathedral. A new word was invented – to coventrate. A new city, with the new cathedral, was started after the war. Blackened ruins of the old cathedral form the approach, with a cross made of two charred roof timbers on the old altar, inscribed 'Father Forgive'. By steps leading to the entrance are two Epstein bronzes of St Michael and of Evil. Inside magnificent stained glass windows by modern artists all lead the eye to a massive block of stone altar surmounted by Geoffrey Clarke's abstract in metal of Cross and Crucified. Behind is the superbly coloured, brilliantly designed 75-ft high tapestry by Graham Sutherland, of the 'Redeeming Saviour of the World'. The Chapel of Unity has a theme of racial and religious understanding. The Chapel of Christ the Servant has a theme of Coventry's industrial plants. Both racial understanding and Coventry's industry are, alas, going through a lean time.

ROMAN CAMP

**Roman Camp Hotel
Callander, Perthshire,
Scotland FK17 8BG (enter the
drive from A84).
Telephone: Callander (0877)
30003.
DBB C;
SBB B.
Dinner C;
lunch A.
Closed end-November to mid-
February.
No credit cards.**

Nose your way between two
pink cottages in Callander's
Main Road and up a narrow
drive to the garden wall and
Roman Camp will come as a
complete surprise. With con-
ical towers topped with grey
tiles and steep roof with dor-
mers, it looks like a small
château in the Dordogne or
Quercy, especially from the
back. The Scottish touch is the
pink-wash, symbol of old
Jacobin sympathies.

Built in 1625 on the site of a
Roman fort beside the river
Teith as a hunting lodge for the
Earls of Mar, it belonged later
to various Lords and Ladies,
including Viscount Esher, con-
fidant of Prime Ministers and
King Edward VII and George V.
He added the towers (one was a
chapel), library and drawing
room and he and his Belgian
wife created the garden, which
is one of the joys of hiding
away in this haven in the wild
hills of central Scotland. A
Lady Wilson made it an hotel
in 1938. Sami Denzler, a Swiss,
and his Ulster-Scottish wife
came from their Edinburgh restaurant 'Denzlers' in 1982.

The bar-lounge and fine panelled library are comfortably
informal, with antiques and
objets d'art the Denzlers have
collected personally over
years. The drawing room overlooking the river is beautiful
but formal, like a picture from
'Homes and Gardens'.

You could believe that the
dining room, with light wood
walls and furniture, low copper lamps, big windows and
painted ceiling was of Swiss
Alpine inspiration. In fact it is
old Scottish, the ceiling
modelled on a seventeenth
century Scottish painted ceiling motif. The Denzlers also
collect modern Scottish paintings. Pleasant bedrooms with
good, spacious bathrooms.

The grounds are a little
heaven, certainly as I saw them
last in late June with masses of
rhododendrons in gorgeous
bloom and other early flowers
also in spring with masses of
daffodils. As a guest you can
fish free in the river running
along the grounds. The view of
the hotel from the other bank
through the trees is delightful.

Food & Drink

Sami Denzler, who does the cooking with his chef Keith Mitchell (a Scot), changes the dinner menu daily, using as much local produce as possible – Scotch beef and lamb, venison, salmon and crayfish are on the menu fairly regularly. He even fills avocado with smoked Scotch mackerel, and makes a splendid cock-a-leekie soup. So he was put out recently when, after receiving praise for years from gastronomes, a snooty Scottish glossy magazine was less than polite about his cooking and meals.

Perhaps this writer was upset because Sami's menu is in French, with explanatory subtitles in English. Scotland probably produces the world's best potatoes and it is rather leading with your chin to describe them as 'Pommes Nouvelles'. But I am all for him using them to make genuine Duchess potatoes and superb Swiss spatzli. Or perhaps the complaint was against honest Scottish pheasant being served with a sweet and sour honey sauce or Angus fillet steak being stuffed with pâté de foie and served with a Madeira sauce. Or was it that superb hot Apfel Strudel which upset him?

I think that Sami Denzler's cooking is refreshingly different without being eccentric and is pleasantly satisfying without being heavy. And I have heard much the same from Scots, Americans and fellow Sassenachs. But not from slimmers.

His sweets are Swiss, not slimming. He is certainly not afraid of using cream. What Swiss worth his salt would be?

The wine list is refreshingly different, too. It starts with four Swiss wines – refreshing and fine for lapping in litres. Next, Australian, at very reasonable prices. Try the Mount Pleasant Chardonnay. Very fair value.

Next come Californian. A few Californian wines are excellent and a lot of rough, mediocre wines live on their deserved reputation. The Cabernet Sauvignon 1979 from Alexander Valley on this list is one of the best – and expensive.

The cheap Austrian wines are for quaffing liberally, too, but not the green Veltliner, or you may have a hangover.

The French come last, after

the Italians and Germans. But prices are so reasonable for an hotel of this standard that you might well be tempted by old favourites like a white Châteauneuf-du-Pape, Château Lalande St Julien, a fruity, Château La Lagune 1976 from Haut Médoc or a glorious Château Palmer 1976 from Margaux costing just about the same as the Californian.

LOCAL DRIVES

Callander is a key junction of Scottish touring – a place where roads meet from the Isles, Glencoe, and Oban, Perth, Dundee and Aberdeen, Edinburgh and the borders. A touring centre for the Trossachs; between Highlands and Lowlands, a land of sharp crags, hills of rock and trees, steep streams, moors and glens. It is now also Tannochbrae of TV's Dr Finlay's Casebook, known to millions around the world who have never been there.

From Aberfoyle (10m SW) to Balquhidder (11m N) and the wild hills beyond you can follow the trail of Robert MacGregor (1671–1734) – Rob Roy, called Scotland's Robin Hood and hero of Walter Scott's novel 'Rob Roy'. Others say he was a brigand, cattle thief and protection racketeer whose clan swore on the head of the King's Forester that no one would grass on the murderer.

Road W into Trossachs past Brig o' Turk (6m) leads to Loch Katrine, which inspired Scott's poem 'Lady of the Lake'. The lady was Ellen Douglas, after whom the island is named. The Clan MacGregor used the island from the Middle Ages to the eighteenth century to hide cattle they had rustled from the lowland farms.

Doune Castle (8m SE), partly ruined but the best-preserved fourteenth-century castle in Scotland. Its builder, Duke Albany, Regent of Scotland, almost inevitably got himself beheaded. The Earls of Moray took it over. 'Bonnie Earl of Moray' of the song lived here. Illegitimate son of James V of Scotland, half-brother to Mary, Queen of Scots, he became her friend and adviser, then turned and led an army against her. He, too, was murdered. Present Earl of Moray owns it (castle open April 1–October 30). In Doune park, with eighteenth-century gardens, is a motor museum of the Earl's vintage and veteran cars, including the world's second oldest Rolls-Royce, early Lagonda, Aston Martin, Hispano Suiza, old Bentleys, a gem of a 1925 Citroën 5 and a 1938 Alfa Romeo made for Le Mans 24-hour Race (open April 1–October 30). Stirling Castle (16m) high on a rock, has dominated Scottish history. Wallace got it back from the English in 1297, Edward I retook it in 1304 until Bruce won at nearby Bannockburn in 1314. It became a residence of Scottish Kings, then a barracks (open all year).

Loch Lomond is twenty miles W of Callander.

A haven in the wide Scottish hills.

Seckford Hall

Seckford Hall
Woodbridge, Suffolk IP13 6NU
(just off A12 from Martlesham
Heath, miss Woodbridge
turning; sign then on left).
Telephone: Woodbridge
(03943) 5678.
DBB C;
SBB B.
Dinner card (average B–C);
lunch A.
Closed Christmas Day.
Children welcome.
Dogs not allowed in any
eating rooms.
Credit cards: Euro, Visa,
Amex, Diners.

I could spend hours sitting among the roses in the sheltered sun-trap garden of this glorious Elizabethan house, drinking cold white wine and watching the ducks coming and going on the lake where Elizabethan gallants took their ladies for rides in punts. Come to think of it, I have!

I feel at home here. Michael Bunn's father bought it in 1950 when it had been an hotel only a short time, and Michael runs it superbly. Despite inevitable internal alterations, it remains to me an Elizabethan Hall where the spirits of former owners still pervade the rooms and corridors.

Some say that Elizabeth I once held court here. Sir Thomas Seckford, who built it in 1530, held the high office of 'Master of the Court Requests'. It is a gorgeous house in red-brown brick, ivy clad, set in thirty-four acres ranging from fine lawns and flower beds to the tree-lined lake, copses, a rough steep hillside thick with rabbits, and a big kitchen garden protected by old brick walls.

Inside the lovely rooms are rich in heavy oak beams, linen-fold wall panels, impressive carved doors and great stone fireplaces. The lounge, the old Great Hall, is superb, but must have been magnificent with its original minstrels' gallery and rafter ceiling right into the roof. Sir Roger Harwood, who made it into an hotel, changed it to make more bedrooms upstairs, which is why my modern bathroom had a Tudor beam carved with the fleur-de-lys and rose of England and more beams patterned the simple white walls of my comfortable single bedroom.

The Bunns found the minstrels' gallery in a garage and moved it to the fine new Lakeside Banqueting Room which looks like part of the original building.

Furnishings are nearly perfect, even in the cosy bar — lovely pieces, much Elizabethan, mostly period, some originally from Windsor Castle. I covet many of them. Bedrooms vary in size and furnishings, most have antiques with one massive four poster; a few are more modern.

Food & Drink

The tank of live lobsters in the hallway, fresh from Aldeburgh, would tempt all but the allergic, and the prices are fair, too.

Chef John Heeley, here for twenty-five years already, favours strongly local products, such as free-range Norfolk ducklings and turkeys, Suffolk chickens, sole, sprats, mussels, plaice from the local coast, vegetables and soft fruit from the walled kitchen garden and even local elderberry wine to soak the melon.

Eating here is not a grand occasion but a nice relaxed friendly way of life. Though not Elizabethan, the serving wenches are comely, friendly of countenance and speech, and willing of service. They are a credit to themselves and Michael Bunn. But these Suffolk girls are too fast for me. I had to ask them to slow down, as I like to take time over my meals.

There is no set-price menu. You choose from a card with prices reasonable but not cheap. Interesting starters include smoked salmon from Orford, cocktail of local crab, a good hors d'oeuvre including prawns and smoked salmon, and a pancake filled with duck, celery and onion. What a joy to see North Sea sprats on a top hotel menu! Food snobs may sneer at sprats. Aristocratic cats and gastronomes know better.

Apart from lobster, the fish choice is difficult – fresh Dover sole, Lowestoft plaice, salmon, trout, and a very tasty pie of lemon sole, prawns and mushrooms in creamy wine sauce with a crisp pastry top.

The chicken breasts in cider, Calvados and apple sauce and cream is called 'Suffolk farm style'. Also, perhaps, Kent, Somerset and Norman style! What's in a name – even the Welsh rarebit with which you could finish.

A sensible choice of wines. Clarets from a very fruity Côtes de Blaye (the unfashionable bit) at £7 (1985) to fine second growth Leoville-Barton 1975 at around £30. A range of Burgundies, but also some nice French regional wines, such as Moulin des Costes from Bandol in the far South of France – wine with flavour and richness almost too easy to drink in that climate, and red Belingard Bergerac, nearest area to Bordeaux, which may not be quite in the Bordeaux class but costs half the price on this list. At double that price is a rarish and lovely white wine – Hermitage Tour Blanche, dry, fine flavour and bouquet and the body of a heavier white Burgundy. Well worth trying. Very nice with lobster.

Sitting in the garden watching the ducks I drink the grapey flavoured, clean-tasting Muscadet Domaine des Dorices. Mind you, if anyone offered me the Saran Natur still Champagne, I would accept. Moët et Chandon give it to me when they invite me to their Château de Saran for lunch!

LOCAL DRIVES *Woodbridge is no longer the picturesque, sleepy place artists flocked to paint as I knew it when young. Still attractive, with its Dutch gabled Shire Hall (another Seckford house), magnificent parish church, and steep streets down to the river Deben, with boatyards which once built a fighting ship for Drake and the 1790s whiteboard tide mill, back in working order. But it draws many tourists in season. And the pleasure yachting boom has brought the boatyards and the quayside chandlers back to life, while yachts of all types line the quay or lie in the mud awaiting the tide. Thirteen miles down river at the sea is Felixstowe, seaside resort since 1900, thriving commercial and passenger port, with a ferry to Zeebrugge in Belgium (some day trips).*

Ipswich (8m SW on A12) is Suffolk's county town on the river Orwell; twelve miles from the open sea but an important port, especially for timber and grain. About fifteen miles SW of Ipswich is the 'Constable Country', where John Constable did much of his painting. He was born at East Bergholt in 1776, son of

the miller of Flatford Mill which he painted (now a National Trust field studies centre). The mill and nearby Willy Lott's Cottage are much as he painted them. Pilgrims pack East Bergholt in season. Dedham nearby was where he painted the mill and the church spire several times. Sir Alfred Munnings, painter of horses, lived in Castle House, now a museum. It contains much of his work including landscapes, gypsies, little known, very pleasant pictures he painted in Paris, and advertising posters for chocolate.

Norwich (50m N – Norman cathedral) – see Congham Hall Hotel, page 43.

Aldeburgh (17m NE on coast) – delightful; Georgian and earlier houses, settled since Saxon times; half-timbered Moot Hall (1512) where local council still meets. Birthplace in 1754 of poet George Crabbe. Benjamin Britten based his opera Peter Grimes on a Crabbe poem. Memorial window to Britten in church by John Piper. Britten directed the music festival for thirty years until he died in 1976. Good fishing from shore. Snape Maltings (12m NE of Woodbridge) a red brick building restored to its original Victorian style after destruction by fire in 1969. This had been converted in 1967 into concert hall for Aldeburgh Festival and is now once again in use; sculptures by Henry Moore and Barbara Hepworth on the lawns.

Sip wine on the lawns where Good Queen Bess trod.

Sharrow Bay

Sharrow Bay Hotel
Lake Ullswater, Penrith,
Cumbria CA10 2LZ
(2m S of Pooley Bridge –
7m on A592 to Penrith;
5m from exit 40 on M6).
Telephone: Pooley Bridge
(08536) 301.
Dinner, bed and breakfast
only
C–D per person.
Dinner E;
lunch D.
Closed early December–early
March.
No children under 13.
No credit cards.

There will never be another hotel like Sharrow Bay. A gorgeous position, perfect hotel-keeping, delectable food with embarrassing choice, old English furniture and English artistry and eccentricity. You will be well cared-for and cossetted.

Another hotel-keeper told me that once you have stayed there, you will remember it for life. Francis Coulson, chef patron, bought this 1840s stone house with half a mile of Ullswater Lake shore in 1949. Brian Sack joined him three years later and they have lost nothing of their care and enthusiasm. It is *not*, as some have said, the

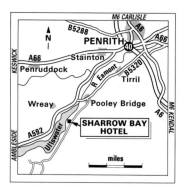

prototype of the English country house hotel, which has existed for over 100 years. It is a house party of paying guests left over from more settled days when guests, fairly formally attired, all met for an aperitif before dinner, drifted into the dining room together around 8 o'clock at the host's request, and were served by staff in starched white jackets with a feast of heroic proportions.

The view down the lake to the fells is an instant cure for motorway madness. The garden is a glorious picture of bright flowers and clipped hedges. The lounges have old-world comfort with plump chairs. Two dining rooms are both delightful. The touch of eccentricity is in the bedrooms. All have fine antique furniture, displays of beautiful china and ornaments, well-chosen drapes and carpets, books, hairdryer, TV, radio and telephone. They vary enormously in size, seven do not have their own bathrooms, and more than half are not in the house. Those who book for longest are likely to get lake views. Some rooms are in

cottage in the grounds, some in an Edwardian lodge, some a mile away in a gorgeous seventeenth-century farmhouse where a truly delightful refectory dining room with minstrels' gallery is used for breakfast. Others are in a pretty village four miles away in an eighteenth-century Quaker cottage with pretty gardens. Some guests choose this for complete tranquillity.

Little touches make this hotel so different – a lovely antique carriage clock in our bedroom, for instance; early morning tea served in Minton china; homemade biscuits in antique containers. And the natural, quiet charm of Francis and Brian, still known after 35 years to their friends as 'the boys from Sharrow'.

Food & Drink

Menus from Sharrow Bay are some of my favourite reading. But do not tarry too long before dinner reading the starters or you will suffer agonies of indecision. I want them *all*. It is easier for Barbara, who is such an addict of marinaded salmon and duck breast that the decision narrows. She will have smoked breast of duck with sauce vert, gravlax of salmon or most likely cebiche of salmon marinaded in walnut oil, lemon juice and wine, with orange and lemon rind. First choice is usually three soups, including a real consommé, and cream of lemon (made also

with onions), one of Chef Francis Coulson's prides and quite delicious, and something more exotic such as soup of mushroom, walnut, orange and tomato. He makes a delightful quiche with chicken, gruyère cheese and broccoli, lighter-than-air cheese choux puffs, and cooks fresh prawns in white wine and cream with tarragon and vegetables.

There is a fish course, often Aberdeen sole, such as sole with salmon mousseline glazed with hollandaise cream sauce. Then a fresh fruit sorbet.

The main course choice is always excellent. Francis cooks at least one roast midday and another in the evening. At dinner recently we were offered roast loin of spring lamb, off the bone, stuffed with chicken mousseline, served with onion tartlet, a pastry dariole of aubergines, courgettes and tomatoes, and lamb gravy with Marsala. Added to this were were the vegetable dishes – mange-tous, broccoli, young carrots and courgettes and potatoes cooked three ways (steamed new, parisienne and Anna, which is thinly sliced and cooked in layers with butter). Alternatives were Cumberland lobster thermidor, local salmon cooked in pastry, roast wild duck with a sauce of Burgundy, cream and peppercorns, local veal filled with pâté and julienne of vegetables with two sauces – Madeira and truffles, watercress and chives, special chicken and calf's liver dishes. Or you could choose from a cold table with ham, tongue and four roasts.

Francis Coulson is inventive but not a 'Nouvelle' chef. Some people have complained about large portions. Silly! You do not have to pick the heaviest dishes or take mountains of vegetables. Nor do you have to choose old English sweets, like butterscotch cream pie or hot sticky toffee sponge. A trolley of beautiful confections is shown to you as you enter the dining room and you could choose the Old English Regency Syllabub or light sour cream flan with strawberries. Cheese is served as a separate course – mostly English cheeses.

The meal costs a lot of money but is worth it for such a feast.

Wines are very suitably varied in type and price and it would be difficult not to find one which pleased your palate, your choice of meal and your bank manager. There are fourteen Bourgeois growth clarets from £7–£40, thirteen excellent, beautifully chosen classified clarets from £20–£100 a bottle, and four 'Grands Crus', including 1961 wines of Château Margaux, Mouton Rothschild and Lafite for a little under £400 a bottle. Nectar, no doubt, but whoever pays that for a bottle of wine?

Although great winesmen do not regard Martillac-commune Graves as top grade, the 1975 Smith-Haut-Lafitte is rich and would suit the lamb with Marsala sauce. With more delicate dishes I would pick La Lagune 1978, a year when this wine has lovely perfume, fine flavour and is smooth.

Among white wines, there is a most pleasant Grand Cru Chablis – a Bourgos by Pierre Henson.

For an aperitif, elevenses (or even for breakfast), this might be your last chance to try Pimm's No3 (the brandy version). It has not been made for several years but the boys from Sharrow wisely got in a stock.

All Lakeland is within easy exploring distance. For information on Ullswater, Lake Windermere, Ambleside (for National Park Information Centre), Grasmere, Wordsworth's houses, see entry for Old Church Hotel, Watermillock, page 108, which you can see across Ullswater.

For information on Keswick, Bassenthwaite Lake and Derwent Water, see Underscar Hotel, page 151.

You can see Ullswater and sometimes Scotland from Penrith Beacon, 5m NE and 937ft high. There is a tower on top, built in 1719. In the public park at Penrith are ruins of a fourteenth-century castle of the Earl of Westmorland, built as a defence against the Scots who raided this area for three centuries until 1603. There are many Wordsworth connections with Penrith. His grandfather William Cookson was a mercer there and William and Dorothy, when staying with him, attended Dame Birkett's Infant School.

At Pooley Bridge (2m N of Sharrow Bay) you can hire boats to explore Ullswater or for fishing. 2m W is Dalemain, a fine mediaeval, Tudor and Georgian house and gardens open to the public.

Delightful welcome, delectable food, unique atmosphere.

Simonsbath

Simonsbath House
Simonsbath, near Minehead,
Somerset TA24 7SH (on B3223
Dulverton–Lynmouth road).
Telephone: Exford
(064 383) 259.
DBB D;
SBB B;
short break reductions.
Dinner B, C.
Closed weekdays November–
February.
Open Christmas and New
Year.
No children under 10.
No dogs.
Credit cards: Euro, Visa,
Amex, Diners.

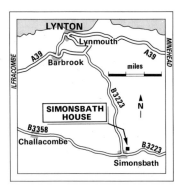

A haven in wild winter weather, a splendid summer or autumn springboard for exploring Exmoor on foot or by car, it is truly an hotel for all seasons. We have relished its log fires, its cosy comfort and warm welcome after a drive through a blizzard and ice-walled lanes and its restful décor, quiet garden and superb food after a hot day's tramping over the ups and downs of wild Exmoor. A pity that it opens only weekends in mid-winter.

It was the first house built on Exmoor, for the first Warden, in 1654 and was the only one until 1815 when the Knight family who lived here built up a village and tried to tame the moor, introducing also new breeds of sheep and horses. Later it was a hunting lodge of Lord Fortescue. The Browns have made a wonderful job of refurbishing it since 1979. Archie was an hotel manager, Margaret was an interior and theatre-set designer. His professionalism and her flair make it unique in such beautiful but wild surroundings.

It stands 1,100 feet above the river Barle valley. Downstairs the Fortescue family arms still decorate panelling. Margaret Brown designed the rest. In the bright attractive dining room in blue and white, you eat off bone china and drink from crystal.

Bedrooms are all different, all quietly colourful, even the china of the early-morning tea-set matching the décor of each room. Bathrooms are modern, with every detail carefully considered from old English soap to bathrobes. Fabrics and linens are beautiful, fresh flowers are on the dressing table, and on the chest a long list of Exmoor sights and books by authors who have written about the area – Blackmore's *Lorna Doone*, Kingsley's *Westward Ho!*, Williamson's *Tarka the Otter*, Delderfield's *To Serve Them All My Days*, Hardy's *A Pair of Blue Eyes* Tennyson's *Idylls of the King* The Browns will give you routes, maps and information for literary pilgrimages. Personally I need no excuse for exploring beautiful Exmoor not even the search for red deer.

and wild ponies. The deer are elusive, the ponies bold. I was awakened once from an after-lunch sleep by something tugging viciously at my hair. An Exmoor pony had mistaken the blonde locks for hay! Alas, he would not get much of a meal now.

Food & Drink

Margaret Brown became the hotel cook by necessity when the chef fell ill. By hard work, a natural flair and research into cookery books and menus back to Elizabethan days, she has developed her own style of cooking based on traditional English and Scottish, particularly English West Country, and on the old recipes she has researched. She has lectured on old British dishes in Britain and the US.

Her cooking is not for slimmers, but is not heavy. She is not afraid of herbs, spices or aromatic sauces – or Somerset clotted cream. Her dishes are often rich, nearly always delicious and ever interesting. Last time I had devilled crab. The flaked crabmeat was cooked in a sauce of tabasco, French mustard, Worcester sauce, anchovy essence, lemon juice, and double cream, topped with crisply fried breadcrumbs and grated Cheddar cheese. Nobody could say it lacked flavour. And it was only a starter.

My favourite main course is a 1750 recipe from Penzance in Cornwall. She bakes fresh lemon sole from local waters with lemon juice, nutmeg and a little mace, covered with thick

clotted cream and a sprinkling of spring onions.

She makes lovely soups. My favourite is Stilton and celery, made with dry cider, chicken stock and double cream. Then there is summer soup made with young fresh peas, celery, French beans, fennel, onion, cucumber, cauliflower heart and courgette in cream and chicken stock (an eighteenth-century recipe), and a nineteenth-century Cornish soup called Kettle Broth of leeks, mustard and cress and cream.

She cooks salmon steaks Scottish-style in cream and Drambuie.

Delicious vegetable dishes include courgette custard and superb carrot cake.

She has an old recipe for apple crumble, too, flavoured with almonds, spices and brandy. These meals may sound a little too much – but not after stumping the Exmoor hills all day. And if you can't hold out until dinner, she serves a full Somerset cream tea.

The wine list of 77 items is modest, with reasonable prices, and a very fair choice of half bottles. I had a pleasant Pouilly Blanc Fumé with the Penzance lemon sole and there was a wide choice of wines from £5–£7 in 1985. Among dearer reds there is an excellent 1979 Château Chasse-Spleen. This is the best wine of Moulis, the area inland from Margaux, producing firm, fruity wines just a little rougher than Margaux itself.

 To explore Exmoor National Park properly you must ultimately get out of your car and walk. There are more driveable lanes and tracks around Brendon Hills in the east than near Simonsbath and Exford in the middle. The Park covers 265 square miles of most varied scenery, with steep hills, steep streams and high ridges covered with bracken and heather, wooded ravines, lonely farms, tens of thousands of Exmoor horn and Devon Closewool sheep, horned Devon red cattle, and the ponies and red deer, both directly descended from prehistoric animals.

Dunster (NE edge of Exmoor Park), old wool market and weaving town with an old dormered Yarn Market, has a red sandstone castle with towers and battlements on a site where castles have stood for 1,000 years, though this one was much reconstructed last century. It has superb staircase, halls and dining room. A very interesting watermill still operates. The Luttrell Arms, an inn built around 1500, has a superb Great Hall.

Places to see on or around Exmoor include Doone Valley (Badgworthy Valley) reached only on foot three miles from Oare – valley of the cut-throat outlaw Doone family in Blackmore's novel. At Oare is the restored church where Lorna Doone married John Ridd and Carver Doone shot at her in the story.

Dunkery Beacon (10m E of Simonsbath by B3223, B3224 to Dunkery Gate, then 3m return walk) is the highest point on the Moor, 1,707ft. Exford, attractive village, is headquarters of the stag hunt.

Lynton and Lynmouth, two small coastal towns at the top and foot of 500ft cliffs, are joined by a cliff railway at a gradient of 1:75. Lynmouth is an old style fishing village of stone houses, some thatched, which survived the 1952 flood disaster when the river Lynn swept through the town. 1½m E by A39 from Lynton, then a short walk is Watersmeet, spectacular meeting place of East Lyn river and Hoar Oak Water in a deep wooded valley. At Heddon's Mouth (5m W of Lynton to Hunter's Inn, then 3m return walk through woods) the river Heddon flows through rock walls up to 700ft before meeting the sea in a small pebble bay.

Porlock has attractive narrow winding streets, a yacht harbour (Porlock Weir) 2m NW, but gets crowded in summer. Porlock Hill (1 in 4) was used for early motor trials.

Tarr Steps (S of Simonsbath) is a remarkable clapper bridge over river Barle from the early Middle Ages – 180ft causeway of flat stones laid upon uprights, some stones weighing over two tons.

Winsford (just off B3223 twelve miles SE of Simonsbath) is the most attractive village on Exmoor, with seven bridges, including a packhorse bridge, and a ford, old thatched houses and thatched Royal Oak Inn (from twelfth century). Birthplace of Ernest Bevin, Trade Union leader and Labour Cabinet Minister under Churchill and Attlee.

Delicious old-time dishes back to Elizabethan Engla...

**The Underscar Hotel
Applethwaite, Keswick,
Cumbria CA12 4PH
(just north of Keswick is a
roundabout where A66 meets
A591; take A591 towards
Carlisle for 30 yards,
then turn right).
Telephone: Keswick (0596)
72469.
DBB B–E;
SBB B.
Dinner C.
Closed over Christmas.
Credit cards: Euro, Visa.**

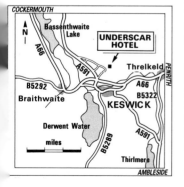

This little hotel hidden in peace in its own estate away from the hurly-burly of Keswick is on its way up in the charts. It has been completely and beautifully refurbished and redecorated, has enthusiastic and professional new owners, management and chef. The grandiose Italianate house, built in 1860 as the country mansion of a magnate, is featured in Pevsner's *Buildings of England*. It is in a magnificent position in forty acres of formal gardens, grass and woodlands, with lovely long views across Derwentwater to the fells. It is half way up the slopes of Skiddaw, one of Britain's highest mountains, which climbs to 3,054 feet above Derwentwater and Bassenthwaite Lake.

Some bedrooms are much smaller than others but have been particularly nicely furnished and decorated in colour themes. The Victorian furnishings are tasteful and without typically Victorian clutter. All rooms have bathrooms.

The Victorians designed fine conservatories, and there is a charming large one here in which we had lunch on our last visit. On nice days it is used for breakfast and tea, too. High above the entrance hall around a skylight is a typically-Italian frieze of nymphs representing the four seasons. The main lounge has huge bay windows from floor to the high ceiling, giving magnificent views. The grounds are a joy.

The manager, David Naylor, spent six years at Sharrow Bay Hotel at Ullswater and one year helping John Tovey to run Miller Howe at Windermere, the highly-individualistic hotel which would undoubtedly have been among my choices if the whole world did not seem to know it already and to have booked the rooms so far ahead. So you can tell that from now on Underscar will be no run-of-the-mill country hotel.

For fishermen, there are fishing rights for trout in Watendlath Tarn.

*A small hotel
with a big future.*

Food & Drink

Chef Clive Wheeler, who came from Langdale Chase Hotel at Windermere, has a praiseworthy aim – to revitalise old British dishes, way back to Queen Elizabeth I's table. But he is introducing the dishes gradually, alongside classic English roasts of sirloin of beef and shoulder and leg of lamb, local salmon in pastry with a lovely creamy, herby Messine sauce.

Among his old-style dishes are lamb with apricot and almonds, Elizabethan pork, English carrot pudding and an old local delicacy of Cumbria, pike and perch pie. Our ancestors thought even more of these two fish than the French do now. He makes a tart of guinea fowl with rosemary as a starter and for sweets an old-fashioned treacle tart and a fine apple pie with almond pastry.

Dinner is a set meal of five courses, with a choice of four dishes on the first, main and sweet course, and is excellent value. The menu is changed daily.

It is a good, varied wine list for a small hotel and by the time you read this will include comments by an expert. There is a 1973 La Lagune third growth Lundon claret at just over £20 which is not cheap but way below the average for this splendid wine. What a lovely wine to drink with the roasts, especially beef! Down to earth, the 1983 Côte de Brouilly from Georges Duboeuf is just the age to have got rid of its earthiness but kept its fruity taste. Perhaps the best bargain among cheaper reds is an 1981 Gigondas which has had time to build up its fruity flavour.

Among whites, there is a Châteauneuf-du-Pape. It is a fairly rare wine and well worth tasting. It has enough body to be drunk right through the meal.

 Keswick is one of the best centres for seeing the Lakes. In summer the Tourist Information office is in the Moot Hall, Market Square (tel: Keswick 72803), in winter in the Keswick council offices (tel: Keswick 72645). The Moot Hall was built in 1813 on the site of a sixteenth-century original. Keswick has been a holiday resort since the Lakeland Poets made the area suddenly fashionable in Victorian times. The Fitz Park museum in Station Road has original manuscripts by Ruskin, Wordsworth and others. The art gallery attached includes works by Turner. The poet Robert Southey was buried in 1843 in Great Crosthwaite churchyard, NW of the town. He lived in Greta Hall. Lovely walks here: Castle Head (National Trust), a 529-ft hill S of Keswick, gives glorious views of Derwentwater and Bassenthwaite Lake; Latrigg, 1,203ft one mile NE gives wider views. Wooded shores of Derwentwater are a photographer's paradise. At Grange (S end of the lake) a lovely old stone bridge crosses a narrow point among fells called the Jaws of Borrowdale. From here take B5289 through Honister Pass (gradient 1 in 4) to Buttermere, a lovely valley with one and a quarter mile long lake hemmed in by mountains. You can walk round the lake. From the tiny church in Buttermere village a path leads to Sour Milk Gill waterfalls. Drive on to Crummock Water, a beautiful two and a half mile long lake. Across it is Scale Force, 100-ft waterfall. Reach B5292 at High Lorton and continue to Cockermouth, ancient town with a ruined castle from 1134 (with dungeons) and Wordsworth House (National Trust), the lovely home where the poet William Wordsworth was born in 1770. Rooms are furnished in the style of his time. In the old kitchen you can taste home baking and have a drink (open April 1–end of October, except Thursday). Moorland Close, farmhouse one and a half miles S of Cockermouth, was the birthplace in 1764 of Fletcher Christian, leader of the mutiny on the Bounty.

Take A591 N from Underscar to Bassenthwaite, then a small road for eight miles NE to Caldbeck, a delightful little village, with a picturesque arched footbridge over the beck (stream) and a twelfth-century church. Near the church door is an elaborate headstone carved with hunting horns to John Peel, who lived here 'once on a day'.D'ye ken him? Born here in 1776, he eloped to Gretna Green with his girl friend, fathered thirteen children

between hunting his own pack of hounds at every opportunity, mostly on foot but later on a horse. And a fall from a horse killed him in 1854 when he was 78. His friend John Graves wrote the words of the song about him.

Halfway down Bassenthwaite Lake is Mire House, lovely seventeenth-century manor connected with Bacon, Wordsworth and Tennyson; original furniture and paintings; grounds to lake. Open April–October.

For more Lakeland sightseeing, see Sharrow Bay Hotel, Ullswater, page 144, and Old Church Hotel, Watermillock, page 108.

Weston Manor Hotel
Weston on the Green,
Oxford OX6 8QL
(8m N of Oxford on A43
Northampton road).
Telephone: Bletchington
(0869) 50621.
DBB D;
Suite E;
SBB B;
many cheaper short breaks.
Dinner B–D.
Open all year.
Credit cards: Euro, Visa,
Amex, Diners.

There are so many fine old houses in Britain that we can become unimpressed by the impressive. Weston Manor, fourteenth-century, is dignified and impressive from the outside, a revelation within. It has literally been in the wars, but is mainly unscathed and looks as if it will stand there among its lawns, topiary hedges and eleven acres of garden forever.

It was a monastery until Henry VIII inevitably dissolved it. Its heated swimming pool is in the monastery garden and the ghosts of monks must be more than impressed by some of the bikini girls besporting themselves.

Being only eight miles from Oxford (Charles I's headquarters) it was also inevitably involved in the Civil War. The foppish and ostentatious Prince Rupert of the Rhine and his cavalry were routed by Cromwell's troops at nearby Islip. Rupert was hidden in a Weston Manor chimney, which must have ruffled the ornate laces he wore even in battle. Cromwell's General Fairfax billeted his officers in the Manor and himself slept in the room where Rupert was hidden. When he left next day, Rupert fled to Oxford, disguised as a dairy maid.

The entrance hall to the Manor is a joy – large, with a fine ceiling, a Tudor fireplace where logs burn in winter, an old Parliament clock and a fine, solid fifteenth-century refectory table. The dining room is grandiose – the old Great Hall of the Manor, 42ft by 19ft, with a minstrels' gallery and fine linenfold panelling all round the room to a height of twelve feet. Bedrooms are nearly all large and the one we used recently was huge. Twin beds with canopies and hangings, a chaise-longue and massive wardrobe seemed quite lost in it.

The grounds are made for wandering, dallying and intrigue, with a rose garden and little paths hidden by sculptured hedges and bushes. It is a fine retreat from a tiring day's stumping round Oxford, exploring the Cotswolds or the Thames Valley.

Food&Drink

The set menu dinner is very good value. Since he took over, Dudley Osborn, the owner, and his chef Nigel Bradbury have been trying to improve the meals without adding greatly to the cost, and they are succeeding. There are usually four choices on each of the three courses and the dishes are changed daily. But there is nearly always a fresh roast of lamb, beef or pork and sometimes Aylesbury duck as well, served with delicious blackcurrant sauce. One simple but tasty starter recently was egg baked with prawns and a cream and cheese topping.

There are some more enterprising dishes on the card. You choose from a long list of starters and main dishes, and pay according to your main dish. Nigel Bradbury serves fresh river trout several ways, including a starter of potted trout with green peppers, served with hot toast and horseradish sauce. Or he cooks them with shallots in rosé wine, then reduces the cooking liquid and adds it to hot hollandaise sauce mixed with double cream.

Barbara tried lobster croquettes of diced lobster in a cream and Swiss cheese sauce, laced with brandy, coated in breadcrumbs and fried. She felt that the cheese and brandy rather overpowered the lobster. But Nigel makes two mouthwatering starters from fresh salmon – one potted in a savoury fish jelly with green peppercorns and lemon, the other sliced thinly, coated with dill sauce, and layered between puff pastry.

There is usually a choice of several beef dishes.

There are more than fifty table wines, mostly moderately priced and fairly simple, including three very cheap, perfectly drinkable house-wines. Barbara found a good, medium priced dry St Veran among the white Burgundies. This appellation was created in 1971, and the wine is regarded as a slightly cheaper substitute for nearby Pouilly-Fuissé, but the wines I have tasted have been drier. Oddly, the red made in the same area is called Beaujolais.

Have you tried, on Spanish holidays, the classic Rioja Marquès de Riscal, regarded as rather pricey in Spain? A fruity, fairly light claret-style wine with a good flavour, it is on this list at a price reasonable by our standards, and would go well with any of the beef dishes.

For a really good red I recommend Château Rauzan Gassies 1975, a fruity wine. It becomes smooth and silky with age, although the 1976 is a better wine.

Although you will not have a true gastronomic meal with great wine here, the food is fresh, the cooking good and the wines sensibly priced, and that is just what most people seek. I think Weston Manor will become very popular for bargain quality short breaks in a distinguished, historic house set in beautiful grounds. *Take a dip in the Monastery Garden*

LOCAL DRIVES *Oxford: few cities give greater rewards for time and study, and Oxford deserves both. If your stay is short, here are places particularly worth visiting: Magdalen College (most beautiful college, where great men including Cardinal Wolsey to Oscar Wilde studied; grounds to the river Cherwell); riverside Botanic Gardens opposite Magdalen; Broad Walk through riverside meadows; Pembroke College (seventeenth-century quadrangle); Christ Church (largest college; superb quad, tower designed by Wren to hold the bell Great Tom; splendid art gallery); Merton College (oldest library in Britain; thirteenth to fourteenth century glass in chapel); All Souls (set up as a memorial to English soldiers killed at Agincourt in 1415; Wren was a fellow of All Souls); Museum of History of Science (scientific instruments, including astronomical); Ashmolean Museum (remarkable collection of paintings, sculptures, watches,*

tapestries, musical instruments and jewels back to Alfred the Great); Wadham College (lovely gardens); Bodleian Library (founded 1480, more than three million books include every new English book published). You can get punts on the Cherwell from beside Magdalen Bridge.

Visiting times depend on whether students are 'up' or 'down' (there or not there). Check with Information Centre, Aldate Chambers (telephone 48707) or Thames and Chilterns Tourist Board, 8 The Market Place, Abingdon, Oxford, telephone (0235) 22711.

For Blenheim Palace, Woodstock (home of the Dukes of Marlborough) see Feathers Hotel, Woodstock, page 49.
For Stratford on Avon, see Billesley Manor, Stratford, page 14.
For Warwick Castle and Kenilworth, see Regent Hotel, Leamington Spa, page 134.

Woodford Bridge Hotel

**Woodford Bridge Hotel
Milton Damerel,
Devon EX22 7LL
(on A388 between Bideford
and Holsworthy).
Telephone: (040 926) 481.
DBB C, D;
SBB A; half-board B, C;
off-season cut-rates;
children up to 10 half-price.
Dinner B, C;
special seasonal menus D, E.
Open all year.
No credit cards.**

A beautiful white fifteenth-century thatched drovers' inn has matured into a beautifully-run three star hotel with several most pleasant surprises. In its twenty acres of delightful gardens and wild nature reserve, rich in rarer birds, are luxury white cottage suites. Each is self-contained, with its own patio, and cleverly designed so that no window overlooks a neighbour. Across a charming little lake, camouflaged by old trees, is a leisure centre with two squash courts, solarium, young people's play room and skittle alley and a superb big heated swimming pool.

The owner, Roger Vincent, former managing director of a Unilever subsidiary, designed much of this. In the lovely old main building, he designed and built with his own hands the delightful bathrooms which blend with the old bedrooms, many of which have brass bedsteads and antique furniture. There is an old-cottage atmosphere in the rooms, with cunning touches like the hairdryer in each bedroom hidden in a flowery tie bag. It is beautifully warm in winter, with central heating throughout and log fires downstairs.

There are three pleasant lounges with deep armchairs, a residents' bar and a big bar with an eating area open to the public and used by local farmers not only for drinking but for bar meals. There are three little dining rooms, too – one with a small dance floor.

Wandering through the grounds is a peaceful pleasure rare these days. You might see many types of birds from tree creepers to buzzards, dippers and kingfishers. The river Torridge runs in front of the grounds. You can fish here for brown trout or, a few miles away on the Upper Torridge, Roger has a run where you can fish in season for salmon and salmon trout. At night you might well find him fishing alongside you. Last year he showed one guest an enormous sea trout which he had caught – then threw it back. 'It was just too beautiful to kill,' he said. But salmon trout is sometimes on the menu.

Food & Drink

One of the river Torridge salmon trout which Roger Vincent did *not* throw back was on the special seasonal Springtime menu on my last spring visit. A thick prime fillet, poached in Muscadet and served with a tomato-flavoured sauce, it would have tempted Achelous, God of the River. Mind you, if you are paying a lot for a meal you expect something extra special. You get it here.

All dishes on this seasonal menu are made from the best local meat, fish and poultry and cooked to order. But you can also get a good cheaper three course meal with coffee. I chose it last time and it was good value. On the main course I was offered a whole Dover sole weighing over 1¼lb, a 1lb-plus T-bone steak, half a duckling served with pineapple and

orange sauce, garnished with fruit (it looked and smelled delicious), two really plump-looking rainbow trout with mushrooms and prawns or an old-fashioned farmhouse grill, with steak, lamb cutlet, liver, bacon, sausages, and onion rings, which looked big enough to satisfy a shot-putter.

I chose Garrick steak. It was two great thick cuts of Devon fillets sandwiching a filling of chopped onions, hams, herbs and mushrooms, wrapped in bacon. It was served with parsley butter, was succulent and cooked exactly to my order. And it was too big for me. The hotel's huge, friendly brown Newfoundland called Guinness must have had a tasty addition to supper. But Devon people eat hearty, and I saw no locals heel-tapping.

The fresh vegetables were

delicious. They included fresh, crisp onion rings, creamed parsnips and crisp young French beans.

My starter was a delight – a truly light and fluffy omelette filled with fresh crab from the nearby coast, served with shrimp sauce. If it had been slightly bigger, I could have made a meal of it.

There were three choices other than salmon trout on the seasonal menu. One was breasts of duckling glazed with honey and served with an oyster and ginger sauce. The honey was local, too, but even Devon cannot produce ginger.

The wine list has a reasonable range and is good value. With the first course I had a very fair, cheap Muscadet and I could have chosen a Moreau Chablis for little more. There was a choice of good bargains in reds

For fishermen, trenchermen and all-the-year swimmers!

158 *Woodford Bridge/Devon*

to go with my steak, including a Chianti Classico Melini, a good Spanish Rioja and a strong-man's drink, the alcoholic, irony Hungarian Bull's Blood. The story goes that when the Hungarians were trying to stop the Turks from reaching Vienna, the Hungarian women, seeing their men tiring, brought them local red wine in bulls' heads. The horrified Saracens said: 'They are drinking the blood of bulls.' And they fled! Not being in the mood to fight Turks, I chose a reasonably-priced Lussac St Emilion, a fruity wine from the frontiers of St Emilion, best drunk young. Though I am one of Margaux's many lovers, I somehow resisted a 1962 Brane-Cantenac though its price was low for such a delicious wine. I told myself that I would wait for a chance to taste the 1961, said to be even better.

You are within fifteen miles of the rugged North Devon coast, with cliffs and sand beaches, about thirty miles from the pleasant but hilly resort of Ilfracombe.

Clovelly (10m), a picture-postcard fishing village, has a stepped and cobbled High Street so steep and narrow that it is for pedestrians and pack-donkeys only. According to which way you are facing, it is called Up-a-long and Down-a-long, and the small whitewashed fisher-cottages terraced down the hill have pretty flowered window-boxes. Mentioned in the Domesday Book 900 years ago, it was built mostly in the eighteenth century, but restored superbly by the estate owner Christine Hamlyn from 1884 to 1936. There are still fishing boats in the tiny harbour, Quay Pool, and on the pebble beach. A lovely approach is by a private clifftop toll road, Hobby Drive, with fine coast views. Clovelly is like a film set, and gets crowded in mid-summer.

Bideford (10m N), a port, has a superb and unusual arched bridge. It was built of oak in the thirteenth century, then the timber used as scaffolding for the replica in stone which replaced it in 1460. It is 557ft long with 24 arches. The town was given to the Grenville family by William Rufus, son of William the Conqueror. Through Sir Richard Grenville's colonization of Virginia and Carolina, Bideford had big trans-Atlantic trade links from the sixteenth century to early eighteenth, including tobacco, Newfoundland cod and the export of wool textiles. The art gallery has fine old English pewter and Devon pottery.

The wild moors of Dartmoor and Exmoor are about thirty miles away (see Prestbury Country House Hotel, Bovey Tracey, page 127, and Simonsbath Hotel, Simonsbath, page 148).

WOODHAYES

Woodhayes
Whimple, Nr Exeter, Devon
EX5 2TD (9m NE of Exeter,
minor road off A30).
Telephone: (0404) 822237.
DBB C, D;
SBB B.
Dinner C;
lunch by order B.
Open all year.
No children under 12.
No dogs.
Credit cards: Euro, Visa,
Amex, Diners.

The tiny village of Whimple, among the cider-apple orchards of East Devon, is a delight – an important-looking church, cottages, of which some are thatched, tiny old-fashioned shops, an unspoiled traditional pub selling good filling bar food, and a little railway station. Though wedged between the M5 and the busy A30 and only nine miles from Exeter, it lives a different life, seemingly in a different century. You can get lost in narrow lanes made for horses and carts.

Woodhayes, a truly handsome early Georgian house, is on Whimple's outskirts among

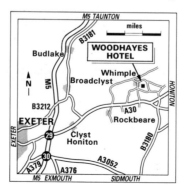

neat gardens and an orchard. You get an uncommonly friendly welcome from John Allen, who in three years has refurbished the rooms charmingly. One of the two lounges is particularly comfortable and home-like, and both have oil paintings, old prints and antiques. The dining room is pleasant. The bedrooms are rather like guest rooms in the home of a discerning friend – freestanding period furniture, matching fabrics, uncluttered, but with everything you need, including mineral water, fresh flowers, up to date magazines and a row of books. I read an old Wisden cricket annual so avidly that I almost missed my pre-dinner glass of Muscadet. Oh, my Lock and my Laker of not so long ago . . .

I find it a delightful centre for exploring Exeter, a fine and interesting city with too many cars and people these days. It is only eleven miles from the coast around Sidmouth and twenty miles from the northeast edge of Dartmoor near Moretonhampstead. There are only seven double bedrooms,

so you must book early. And casual diners not staying will be lucky to find a table.

Food & Drink

Adrian Thompson is a type of British chef I like. No stick-in-the-mud traditionalist, he is progressive but mainly within the limits of the very best fresh local ingredients. Much as I love nearly all French cuisine, and most Italian, I prefer something more local here in Britain. Ingredients are different, so is the climate. French cooking does not travel as well as some food snobs believe.

He offers a four course menu with good choice on each course, and everything is cooked fresh, so meal times are fairly rigid, with one sitting and last dinner at 8p.m. His roast lamb with rosemary sauce is delightful, so is his local trout stuffed with almonds and served with sorrel and prawns.

He does stray a bit out of England. He has a slightly 'Nouvelle' avocado and lemon soup. But I prefer his soup of Devon cider and Stilton. And his poached lemon sole from Torbay thirty-two miles away is delicious served in sorrel and prawn sauce. He makes

very good smoked seafood mousse with fennel sauce as a starter and a very tasty main dish of chunks of local beef flamed in brandy, then served with chicken liver and a red-currant jelly sauce in a puff pastry 'nest'. The combination of beef and chicken liver is an old English idea which we seem to have left to the Italians.

He even makes the biscuits accompanying generous portions of English cheeses.

Wines are sensibly chosen and sensibly priced, and there is a fair choice of half bottles for those of us who like 'half of white, half of red'. Housewines include a white wine from St

Purcain (on a tributary of the Loire, called the Sioule) which I have drunk in the Auvergne. It is made from Chardonnay and Sauvignon grapes, mixed with a local variety, and is fresh and fruity. It makes a good 'starter' wine here. There is also a Frascati from the hills of Rome, but I find that too thin. But for reds there is such a good choice from Beaujolais at such fair prices that it seems a pity not to take advantage of them. They are all there, Brouilly, Juliénas, Fleurie, Moulin-à-Vent, Morgon, Beaujolais Villages, Chiroubles, and most carry the label of the big and very reliable négociant Georges Duboeuf.

Chiroubles is a wine so light, easy to drink and tempting that it has caused many a drinker not to realise that they have had enough. This one is from Château Javernaud. But I like Brouilly, which is fruity and satisfying and cannot be hurried, and there is a very good one here which won a gold medal at Macon wine fair last year, Château des Tours. It would be easy for me to become addicted to Brouilly, with so much Burgundy out of my price range and claret likely to be scarcer after such a thin 1984 harvest.

For a good-value dry white to go with the excellent local fish dishes, there is a 1983 Sancerre by Serge Laporte with a lingering fruity, slightly smokey flavour. John Allen has a good list for those of us whose capacity for wine often exceeds our bank accounts – but he does not ignore serious lovers of such treasures as Grand Puy-Lacoste 1976 Pauillac – a wine for those who like strong flavour which lasts.

A charming hideout off the map.

 Exeter, one of our oldest towns, founded by the Romans 50AD, now a university and cathedral city, was brutally bombed by the Germans in 1942 and its centre destroyed. Happily the cathedral survived. It was built in 1260, using two beautiful transceptal towers from a twelfth-century Norman cathedral. The old town towards the river Exe has many fine old buildings, including the Custom House and a maze of lanes and little streets, with mediaeval inns and little shops. On Town Quay is a fascinating Maritime Museum with over 75 sail, oar and steam-propelled vessels from the past, including an Aráb dhow, Fijian outrigger and a spritsail barge, all in the water.

The modern rebuilt centre is a shopping complex, with decorative pavements, arcades, flower beds and lawns, praised by some locals heartily, disliked by others.

Bicton Park (south, just before Budleigh Salterton) are gorgeous gardens of Lord Clinton's estate, open to the public. The Italian Garden was laid out in 1735 by Le Nôtre, who designed the gardens of Versailles. There is a narrow-gauge woodland railway, children's playground and several museums.

Killerton Gardens (7m NE towards Cullompton road) – Sir Richard Acland, Labour MP, and son of a Liberal cabinet minister, gave the home, gardens and estates which the Aclands had owned since 1778 to the National Trust and became headmaster of a State school. The arboretum is particularly splendid.

Dartmoor – see Prestbury Country House Hotel, Bovey Tracey, page 127.

INDEX OF NAMES AND ADDRESSES

The Airds Hotel
Port Appin, Appin
Argyll
Scotland   PA38 4DF
(063 173) 236

Balcary Bay Hotel
Auchencairn
Near Castle Douglas
Kirkcudbrightshire
Scotland   DG7 1QZ
(055 664) 217

Balcraig House
By Scone
Near Perth, Perthshire
Scotland
(0736) 51123

Banchory Lodge Hotel
Banchory
Kincardine & Deeside
Scotland   AB3 3HS
(033 02) 2625

Billesley Manor Hotel
Billesley
Near Stratford-upon-Avon
Warwickshire   B49 6NF
(0789) 763737

Bishopstrow House
Boreham Road
Warminster
Wiltshire   BA12 9HH
(0985) 212312

Bodysgallen Hall Hotel
Llandudno
Gwynedd
North Wales   LL30 1RS
(0492) 84466

Breamish House Hotel
Powburn
Alnwick
Northumberland
NE66 4EL
(066 578) 266

Burleigh Court Hotel
Minchinhampton, Near
Stroud
Gloucestershire   GL5 2PF
(0453) 883804

Cavendish Hotel
Baslow
Derbyshire   DE4 1SP
(024 688) 2311

Chewton Glen
New Milton
Hampshire   BH25 6QS
(04252) 5341

Clifton Hotel
Viewfield Street
Nairn
Nairnshire   IV12 4HW
(0667) 53119

Combe House
Gittisham, Near Honiton
Devon   EX14 0AD
(0404) 2756

Congham Hall
Grimston
King's Lynn
Norfolk   PE32 1AH
(0485) 600250

Elcot Park Hotel
Elcot, Near Newbury
Berkshire   RG16 8NJ
(0488) 58100

The Feathers Hotel
Market Street
Woodstock
Oxfordshire   OX7 1SX
(0993) 812291

Granville Hotel
St Margaret's Bay, Near
Dover
Kent   CT15 6OX
(0304) 852212

Greywalls Hotel
Muirfield
Gullane
East Lothian
Scotland   EH31 2EG
(0620) 842144

Hackness Grange
Country Hotel
North York Moors
National Park
Near Scarborough
Yorkshire   YO13 0JW
(0723) 69966

Homewood Park Hotel
Hinton Charterhouse
Bath
Avon   BA3 6BB
(022 122) 2643

Hope End Hotel
Hope End, Near Ledbury
Hereford and
Worcester   HR8 1DS
(0531) 3613

Kennel Holt
Cranbrook
Kent   TN17 2PT
(0580) 712032

Kirkby Fleetham Hall
Kirkby Fleetham
Northallerton
North Yorkshire
DL7 0SU
(0609) 748226

Knockinaam Lodge Hotel
Portpatrick
Wigtownshire
Scotland   DG9 9AD
(077 681) 471

Lainston House
Sparsholt
Winchester
Hampshire   SO21 2LT
(0962) 63588

Lamorna Cove Hotel
Lamorna Cove, Near
Penzance
Cornwall   TR19 6XH
(0736) 731411

Linden Hall Hotel
Longhorsley
Morpeth
Northumberland
(0670) 56611

Lords of the Manor Hotel
Upper Slaughter
Near Bourton-on-the-
Water
Cheltenham
Gloucestershire
GL542JD
(0451) 20243

The Lygon Arms
Broadway
Worcestershire   WR12
7DU
(0386) 852255

Maes-y-Neuadd
Talsarnau
Gwynedd
North Wales
(0766) 780200

Meudon Hotel
Mawnan Smith
Falmouth
Cornwall   TR11 5HT
(0326) 250541

Middlethorpe Hall
Bishopthorpe Road
York   YO2 1QP
(0904) 641241

Oakley Court Hotel
Windsor Road, Water
Oakley
Near Windsor
Berkshire   SL4 5UR
(0628) 74141

Old Church Hotel
Watermillock
Penrith
Cumbria   CA11 0JN
(085 36) 204

Palé Hall Hotel
Llandderfel, Near Bala
Gwynedd
North Wales   LL23 7PS
(06783) 285

Pengethley Hotel
Near Ross-on-Wye
Herefordshire   HR9 6LL
(098987) 211

Penmere Manor Hotel
Mongleath Road
Falmouth
Cornwall   TR11 4PN
(0326) 314545

Plumber Manor
Sturminster Newton
Dorset   DT10 2AF
(0258) 72507

Porth Tocyn Hotel
Abersoch
Pwllheli
Gwynedd   LL53 7BU
(075 881) 2966

Prestbury Country House Hotel
Brimley Lane
Bovey Tracey
South Devon   TQ13 9JS
(0626) 833246

The Priory Country House Hotel
Rushlake Green
Heathfield
East Sussex   TN21 9RG
(0435) 830553

Regent Hotel
The Parade
Royal Leamington Spa
Warwickshire   CV32 4AX
(0926) 27231

Roman Camp Hotel
Callander
Perthshire
Scotland   FK17 8BG
(0877) 30003

Seckford Hall
Woodbridge
Suffolk   IP13 6NU
(03943) 5678

Sharrow Bay Hotel
Lake Ullswater
Penrith
Cumbria   CA10 2LZ
(08536) 301

Simonsbath House
Simonsbath
Near Minehead
Somerset   TA24 7SH
(064 383) 259

The Underscar Hotel
Applethwaite
Keswick
Cumbria   CA12 4PH
(0596) 72469

Weston Manor Hotel
Weston-on-the-Green
Oxford   OX6 8QL
(0869) 50621

Woodford Bridge Hotel
Milton Damerel
Devon   EX22 7LL
(040 926) 481

Woodhayes
Whimple
Near Exeter
Devon   EX5 3TD
(0404) 822237

Room and menu grades
DBB Double room and breakfast for 2 people.
SBB Single room and breakfast for one person.
Price codes, including VAT:

Bed & breakfast **Dinner**

Bed & breakfast	Dinner
A under £30	A under £10
B £30–£45	B £10–£13
C £45–£60	C £13–£16
D £60–£75	D £16–£20
E £75–£85	E over £20
F over £85	

Prices are as quoted near the end of 1985. In some hotels there may be special two-room suites at higher prices. Dinner prices are for set-price meals, unless stated. Most hotels also offer à la carte (card) dishes.

Maps
Essential – Ordnance Survey maps: 1:250,000 for hotel area. Or *New Book of the Road* (Reader's Digest/AA). Very useful: Ordnance Survey 1:50,000 map of area.

Books
AA Illustrated Guide to Britain is informative and attractive. *Shell Guide to Britain* is very useful.

Other useful books:
AA Touring Book of Britain
AA Book of British Villages
AA Book of British Towns
AA Illustrated Guide to
  Britain's Coastline
Green Michelin: England –
  The West Country

For current yearly prices, see the AA's excellent *Hotels and Restaurants in Britain* – quite the best guide to hotels in general.